5 Tips for HEALTHY EATING

1 Healthy Choices
(banish the "all or nothing" approach)

2 Eat 6 Times A Day
(cut your 3 meals in half; regulates metabolism & energy, avoids starvation!)

3 Drink Water All Day Long
(nothing works without water; cleanse, shuttle, metabolize)

4 Timing
(limit carbs after lunch; when and what you eat should align with what you are doing)

5 Variety
(cycle variety into your diet; daily and weekly)

Healthy habits last, diets don't. "

Jen ARRICALE™

Love Yourself, Love Your Life, Spread it Around

This book is dedicated to every single
one of you, with the hope that you learn
to love yourself,
love your life,
and spread it around

Healthy Recipes for a Busy Life

Easy to prepare, fun to share!

Jen Arricale
Celebrity Fitness Chef

Sassy Spoon Publishing

Omaha, Nebraska

HEALTHY RECIPES FOR A BUSY LIFE
© 2014 by Jennifer A. Arricale.

Paperback ISBN: 978-0-9916233-1-0
Mobi ISBN: 978-0-9916233-2-7
EPub: 978-0-9916233-0-3

LCCN: 2014903882

Library of Congress Cataloging Data available from Publisher

SASSY SPOON PUBLISHING
www.jenarricale.com

Special thanks to the many that have contributed and supported along the way! Including:
* Kontempo Salon for gorgeous hair and makeup.
* www.kontempoomaha.com
* Richard Lahti for the fantastic cover design.
* John Mazzei for the cover photography, and the majority of food photography adorning this book.
* Christie Toland, NHC, for the nutritional information on each recipe.
* Family and friends for all the encouragement and taste testing.

Printed in the United States of America.

10 9 8 7 6 5 4 3 2 1

Contents

Preface

One of the most amazing insights I've discovered during my personal journey towards health and happiness is realizing just how much my story has in common with that of so many others. We are all striving to overcome doubts, fears, and challenges in order to live a happy, healthy life. We deserve it, and we are worth it! The first step is to take control of our lives. But where to begin?

I think about food and life using these three fundamental principles:

Love yourself – it all starts here. Self-love and self-respect are the cornerstones of a happy, healthy life, and the journey can begin with something as basic as taking control over what you choose to put in your body through the food we eat.

Love your life – it deepens and grows from here. When you feel good about yourself, your life begins to reflect this back to others.

Spread it around – this is where it multiplies and intensifies. Sharing your health and happiness with others is much like serving a great meal: people love it, want more of it, and won't leave without the recipe so they can share it with their friends and family.

Many of us want to live a healthy, empowered life, but simply don't know how. In this book, I share some of my favorite recipes for a delicious, nutritious, and easy solution to eating right no matter how busy your life is. No long preparations, no crazy ingredients, no special tools or appliances. This is real food for real people who want to make a positive change in their health and well-being in order to be the best possible version of themselves. I share your desire, and I applaud you for taking action to make it happen. Thank you for sharing your kitchen with me.

When people get a glimpse of what I do and how I do it, they often comment on my passion, drive and dedication, and then ask what motivates me. My answer: I hope to inspire others to accomplish their dreams through healthy living. And, yes, I believe that starts with good food.

"As in food... so in life."

Introduction

You might think that just because I'm a foodie who likes being fit and healthy that I was always that way. The fact is, for most of my life, I was the opposite.

Growing up in a Bronx suburb, as part of a close Italian family meant big family dinners and celebrations. I loved those times, getting together, laughing and sharing. From my earliest memories, food became a connection to the people I love, and it gave me comfort.

My relationship with food was healthy and normal when my grandmother would prepare homemade meals that were both delicious and nourishing. But when my parents decided to move to Phoenix in search of opportunity, everything changed. In the span of just a few days, I lost my friends, my extended family and my home. Comfort through food became comfort through processed food. And exercise? Well, I didn't even consider it.

My destructive behavior of bad food and no exercise went on into early adulthood along with smoking and drinking. It wasn't until my marriage to my college sweetheart fell apart that I looked in the mirror and realized how far I had fallen. I was unhealthy, overweight, broken, devastated. I realized I could either continue this downhill slide emotionally and physically or make a right turn in my life.

I didn't have much choice. I wanted to live again, and I wanted to feel good again. I wanted to feel good about myself, and good about my life. I set out to learn how to eat right and live on my own. I quit my unhealthy habits and began to learn about taking better care of myself. Eventually I joined a gym and started exercising, and I began experimenting with vegetarian cooking. I felt reborn, and in many ways I was.

In time, exercise didn't feel like exercise. I started hiking, learned my way around the gym and as the years passed, I would learn bits and pieces that became enduring parts of my life. In my late thirties I began tackling bigger and bigger health and fitness goals like running marathons and hiking the Seven Summit Challenge. Through my thirties and early forties, I became purposeful with food by preparing new creations and sharing them with friends. In my mid-forties I discovered competitive natural bodybuilding and ultimately medaled in the Natural Olympia. The joy and comfort of food and family was back in my life. I also discovered how to fit a healthy lifestyle into a busy career and how to create healthy dishes for friends who don't want to eat tofu.

Today, I'm sharing my love for food and togetherness in a very big way. The comfort and joy that sharing great food in my Nana's kitchen with loved ones once gave me as a child is alive in my life today. You can get healthy and fit and still eat great! I'm living proof that it's never too late to decide you are worth it. And you deserve to live a healthy, happy life. Join me in the journey. I'll join you in yours.

LOVE,

Jen

P.S. I have used a few abbreviations throughout the book that I wanted to tell you about:

gf   recipe is gluten-free or can be modified to be gluten free

df   recipe is dairy-free or can be modified to be dairy free

v   recipe is vegetarian or can be modified to be vegetarian

Morning Meals

VEGETABLE & FETA FRITTATA
WITH SHREDDED CHICKEN

SERVES 2-4

I created this for a friend's New Year's Day brunch and it was so fun to share something healthy and delicious with her on the first day of a new year!

INGREDIENTS

1 tbsp	olive oil
½	red onion, finely chopped
1	portabella mushroom, finely chopped
1	marinated roasted red pepper, finely chopped
1 cup	fresh spinach, stems removed and chopped
2 tsp	garlic powder
12	egg whites
½ cup	skim milk
1 cup	low fat cottage cheese
1 tbsp	dried basil
½ cup	reduced fat feta cheese, crumbled
1 tsp	ground paprika
12oz	cooked, seasoned chicken breast, shredded into bite-sized pieces
	freshly ground black pepper, to taste

DIRECTIONS

Heat olive oil in a large non-stick pan. Add chopped vegetables and garlic, sautéing on high for 5-10 minutes, or until vegetables are well cooked and browning. While vegetables are cooking, add egg whites, milk, cottage cheese, basil, and pepper to a mixing bowl and whisk vigorously. Set aside. Transfer sautéed vegetables into bowl with egg, add chicken and return pan to heat. Stir contents of bowl and pour into pan, reducing heat to medium. Cook on medium heat for 10-15 minutes, or until liquid appears to be setting. During last few minutes, sprinkle feta and paprika evenly over top of frittata. Use a spatula to cut the cooking frittata into quarters. Flip each quarter to continue cooking process on other side for another 5 or so minutes until both sides are nicely browned. Flip quarters over (so feta and paprika are on top) and serve immediately with your favorite salsa.

SERVING & LEFTOVER SUGGESTIONS

Eat cold for a high-protein snack, or stuff into a pita pocket and top with a fruity hot salsa for a great lunch.

NUTRITION PER SERVING

281 Calories
41g Protein
9g Fat
8g Carbs
1g Fiber
4g Sugar

gf *v* make without chicken

Eggs in a Blanket

Serves 1

This is one of my all-time favorite creations because it is healthy and versatile! This makes a great lunch, cut up for a snack, or even cold!

INGREDIENTS

6 egg whites
1 whole grain wrap or tortilla
2 tbsp pre-made hummus
½ cup chunky salsa (excess liquid strained off)
½ avocado

DIRECTIONS

Add all egg whites to a lightly oiled or non-stick pan, browning nicely on each side before removing from heat. Lay wrap out flat, spreading hummus and salsa evenly over wrap. Cut egg whites into bite sized pieces and layer onto wrap, topping with sliced avocado. Roll filled wrap and enjoy immediately.

SERVING & LEFTOVER SUGGESTIONS

This is a meal unto itself, so enjoy solo for a hearty breakfast or lunch.

NUTRITION PER SERVING

506 Calories
30g Protein
24g Fat
45g Carbs
10g Fiber
7g Sugar

df v

Fiesta Omelet

Serves 2

This omelet is a Sunday staple around our house! Sometimes we make it without meat, sometimes with, but always with colorful vegetables.

INGREDIENTS

1 tbsp	olive oil
2	fresh jalapeños, stem and seeds removed, finely chopped
1	fresh red bell pepper, stem and seeds removed, finely chopped
1	fresh tomato, chopped
½	red onion, finely chopped
1 4-oz can	green chilies, rinsed and strained
¼ cup	fresh cilantro, stems removed, finely chopped
2 tsp	garlic powder
2 tsp	ground cumin
8	egg whites
1 cup	turkey chorizo sausage or shredded chicken breast, pre-cooked freshly ground black pepper, to taste

DIRECTIONS

Heat olive oil in a large pan. Add all vegetables, herbs, and spices to pan, sautéing on high for 5-8 minutes, or until vegetables are browning and slightly softened. Spread sautéed vegetables evenly over bottom surface of pan, pour egg whites over vegetables, and then evenly cover with cooked meat. Cook on medium high for 8-10 minutes, or until liquid appears to be setting. Use a spatula to cut the cooking omelet into quarters. Flip each quarter to continue cooking process on other side. Cook another 5 or so minutes until both sides are nicely browned. Serve immediately.

SERVING & LEFTOVER SUGGESTIONS

Eat cold for a high-protein snack, or stuff into a pita pocket and top with a fruity hot salsa for a great lunch.

NUTRITION PER SERVING

245 Calories
27g Protein
12g Fat
 9g Carbs
 2g Fiber
 3g Sugar

gf df v make without turkey or chicken

TURKEY & CHEESE OMELET

SERVES 2

*I love making this with whatever leftover meat I have on hand—
anything lean and shreddable is a candidate!*

INGREDIENTS

1 tbsp	olive oil
½	red onion, finely chopped
½ cup	fresh mushrooms, finely chopped
¼ cup	fresh Italian parsley, stems removed, finely chopped
3	fresh basil leaves, finely chopped
2 tsp	garlic powder
1 tsp	paprika
8	egg whites
½ cup	reduced fat Swiss cheese, shredded or cut into thin strips
1 cup	thinly sliced turkey breast, pre-cooked
	freshly ground black pepper, to taste

DIRECTIONS

Heat olive oil in a large pan. Add all ingredients except eggs, cheese and meat, sautéing on high for 5-8 minutes, or until vegetables are browning and slightly softened. Spread sautéed vegetables evenly over bottom surface of pan, pour egg whites over vegetables, sprinkle with cheese and then evenly cover with cooked meat. Cook on medium-high heat for 8-10 minutes, or until liquid appears to be setting. Use a spatula to cut the cooking omelet into quarters. Flip each quarter to continue cooking process on other side. Cook another 5 or so minutes until both sides are nicely browned. Serve immediately.

SERVING & LEFTOVER SUGGESTIONS

Eat cold for a high-protein snack, or stuff into a pita pocket and top with a fruity hot salsa for a great lunch.

NUTRITION PER SERVING

- **409** Calories
- **49g** Protein
- **18g** Fat
- **11g** Carbs
- **2g** Fiber
- **5g** Sugar

gf v make without turkey

YOGURT PARFAIT

SERVES 2-4

Yummy! This is also a great healthy dessert for the entire family. Want fewer calories? Skip the dried apricots.

INGREDIENTS

1 cup	non-fat plain Greek yogurt
1 scoop	vanilla protein powder
1 tsp	cinnamon
½ cup	fresh blueberries (or frozen blueberries thawed)
½	fresh pear, shredded, with skin on
¼ cup	dried apricots, finely chopped
¼ cup	walnuts or almonds, chopped

DIRECTIONS

In a small mixing bowl, stir protein powder and cinnamon into yogurt; mix well. In a tall glass, alternate layers of yogurt mixture with remaining ingredients, ending with fruit and nut combination on top.

NUTRITION PER SERVING

562	Calories
44g	Protein
22g	Fat
56g	Carbs
9g	Fiber
42g	Sugar

gf v

PECAN BANANA PANCAKES

SERVES 4

These taste more like dessert cakes than breakfast!

INGREDIENTS

½ cup	pancake mix
½ cup	vanilla protein powder
1 cup	buckwheat flour
1 tsp	cinnamon
½ tsp	ground cloves
½ cup	applesauce
1	large extra ripe banana, peeled
½ cup	chopped, unsalted pecans
	remaining liquid ingredients called for in pancake mix recipe, less ½ cup

DIRECTIONS

Combine all dry ingredients in a large mixing bowl. Mix in remaining ingredients until well combined. Cook pancakes according to pancake mix instructions, and serve warm.

SERVING & LEFTOVER SUGGESTIONS

Serve with fresh berries or mango. Enjoy leftovers cold without syrup for a sweet, cake-like snack, or spread cold cakes with peanut butter for a high-energy snack.

NUTRITION PER SERVING

290	Calories
19g	Protein
11g	Fat
30g	Carbs
5g	Fiber
7g	Sugar

df v

Power Oats & Berries

Serves 1

I remember the first time I used green tea in place of regular water and loved the extra health benefits it gave without altering the taste.

INGREDIENTS

- **½ cup** old-fashioned or steel-cut oats
- **¼ cup** green tea or water
- **1 tsp** cinnamon
- **¼ cup** fresh or frozen blueberries, thawed
- **2 scoops** vanilla protein powder
- **¼ cup** fresh strawberries, thinly sliced
- **¼ cup** fresh blackberries

DIRECTIONS

Combine first four ingredients in a large mixing bowl, stirring until evenly mixed. Microwave on high, covered, for 2-3 minutes. Remove from heat, mix well, and add protein powder and remaining berries on top.

NUTRITION PER SERVING

- **400** Calories
- **42g** Protein
- **7g** Fat
- **45g** Carbs
- **9g** Fiber
- **13g** Sugar

gf df v

GARDEN EGG WHITE OMELET

SERVES 4

This classic can easily made without the milk and cheese for an option that's even lower in calories and fat.

INGREDIENTS

1 tbsp	olive oil
2	green onions, finely chopped
1	red bell pepper, stem and seeds removed, finely chopped
1 cup	fresh spinach, finely chopped
¼ cup	Italian parsley, finely chopped
2 tsp	garlic powder
½ cup	parmesan cheese, grated
12	egg whites
½ cup	skim milk
1 tbsp	dried basil
	freshly ground black pepper, to taste

DIRECTIONS

Heat olive oil in a large pan. Add chopped onions and bell pepper, sauté on high for 5 minutes, or until vegetables are well cooked and browning. Add chopped spinach, parsley, garlic and pepper, sautéing another 2 minutes. Spread sautéed vegetables evenly over bottom surface of pan, and top with parmesan cheese, sprinkled evenly as well. Vigorously combine egg whites, milk and basil in a large mixing bowl, and then pour contents over vegetable-and-cheese-lined frying pan. Cook on medium-high heat for 8-10 minutes, or until liquid appears to be setting. Use a spatula to cut the cooking omelet into quarters. Flip each quarter to continue cooking process on other side. Cook another 5 or so minutes until both sides are nicely browned. Serve immediately.

SERVING & LEFTOVER SUGGESTIONS

Eat cold for a high-protein snack, or stuff into a pita pocket and top with a fruity hot salsa for a great lunch.

NUTRITION PER SERVING

164 Calories
18g Protein
8g Fat
6g Carbs
1g Fiber
3g Sugar

gf df make without milk & cheese *v*

BAKED OATMEAL SQUARES

MAKES 12 SQUARES

Ever wish you could eat your oatmeal on the go? Well, you can get all oatmeal's power in this baked version. This will appeal to even picky eaters who don't like mushy oatmeal. Paired with lots of fruit, nuts and protein, this recipe may banish mushy oatmeal forever! Enjoy!

INGREDIENTS

1 ½ cups oats
½ cup vanilla protein powder
¼ cup ground flaxseed meal
1 cup water
1 cup fresh or frozen blueberries, thawed
½ cup fresh or frozen mango or peach, thawed and in small pieces
1 overripe banana, mashed
½ cup walnuts, chopped into small pieces
1 tbsp agave nectar or honey
2 tsp ground cinnamon
1 tsp ground cloves
1 tsp pure vanilla extract

DIRECTIONS

Preheat oven to 375 degrees. Combine all ingredients in a bowl and mix well with a fork until batter is moist. Transfer batter into lightly-oiled 9" x 12" baking dish. Bake for 25 minutes.

SERVING & LEFTOVER SUGGESTIONS

Crumble onto low-fat Greek yogurt; add fresh fruit and cinnamon for a delicious parfait.

NUTRITION PER SERVING

127 Calories
8g Protein
5g Fat
15g Carbs
3g Fiber
5g Sugar

gf df v

Blueberry Applesauce
Powercakes

Serves 4

These are my favorite pancakes to enjoy cold....yep, I eat them like soft cookies as an afternoon treat!

INGREDIENTS

1 ½ **cups**	pancake mix
½ **cup**	buckwheat flour
½ **cup**	vanilla protein powder
¼ **cup**	ground flaxseed meal
1 **tsp**	cinnamon
½ **tsp**	ground cloves
½ **cup**	applesauce
½	overripe banana, mashed
½ **cup**	fresh or frozen blueberries, thawed
	remaining liquid ingredients called for in pancake mix recipe, less ½ cup

DIRECTIONS

Combine all dry ingredients in a large mixing bowl. Mix in remaining ingredients (except blueberries) until well-combined, but do not over-mix. Gently fold in blueberries. Cook pancakes according to pancake mix instructions, and serve with warm maple syrup.

SERVING & LEFTOVER SUGGESTIONS

Eat cold without any syrup for a sweet, cakelike snack, or spread cold cakes with peanut butter for a high-energy snack.

NUTRITION PER SERVING

311	Calories
19g	Protein
7g	Fat
46g	Carbs
9g	Fiber
12g	Sugar

PAN-FRIED
SWEET POTATOES & ONIONS

SERVES 2-4

I don't know if I like this dish better warm or cold... or with or without ketchup!

INGREDIENTS

1 tbsp olive oil
1 red onion, finely chopped
2 large sweet potatoes
1 tbsp fresh Italian parsley, finely chopped
1 tbsp garlic powder
1 tbsp ground paprika
freshly ground black pepper, to taste

DIRECTIONS

Heat olive oil in a large pan. Add chopped onion and sauté on medium heat. While onions are cooking, soften potatoes in microwave on high for 4 minutes. Cut slightly softened potatoes lengthwise and then slice into ½-inch pieces, adding to onions in pan. Increase heat to high, add remaining ingredients and sauté another 5-8 minutes or until potatoes and onions are slightly browned. Serve warm, with some ketchup for dipping.

SERVING & LEFTOVER SUGGESTIONS

Serve with any egg dish. Enjoy leftovers by sprinkling a wheat tortilla with cheese, top with potato and onion mixture and cook until cheese is melted. Fold and enjoy.

NUTRITION PER SERVING

121 Calories
2g Protein
4g Fat
21g Carbs
4g Fiber
8g Sugar

gf df v (Note: leftover suggestions are not gf and df)

31

EGG WHITE & AVOCADO

SERVES 1

This simple recipe is easy enough for a workday breakfast but elegant enough for a brunch. I say, enjoy it at both!

INGREDIENTS

6 egg whites
1 tsp black pepper
1 tsp dried basil (or twice as much fresh, diced)
½ avocado
salsa for garnish

DIRECTIONS

Cook egg whites for 2-4 minutes in lightly oiled frying pan on medium heat with spices on top. Fold one half of egg flat over, omelet style, and transfer to plate. Add avocado slices and a dab of salsa on top as a garnish and enjoy!

SERVING & LEFTOVER SUGGESTIONS

Eat cold for a high-protein snack, or stuff into a pita pocket and top with a fruity hot salsa for a great lunch.

NUTRITION PER SERVING

255 Calories
24g Protein
14g Fat
11g Carbs
7g Fiber
2g Sugar

gf df v

What about a *smoothie* for Breakfast?

Flip to page 162 for recipes!

Salads & Vegetable Dishes

Roasted Spicy
Vegetable Stock

Makes approximately 8 cups

This is a great example of investing a little time to make a big pot of goodness that can be enjoyed today and then again and again by freezing small batches.

INGREDIENTS

- ¼ **cup** balsamic vinegar
- ¼ **cup** dry red wine
- ¼ **cup** liquid aminos (or low-sodium soy sauce)
- **2 tsp** olive oil
- **15-20** whole crimini mushrooms
- **3** large carrots, peeled, cut in half and then lengthwise
- **2** medium red onions, peeled and quartered
- **8** garlic clove, peeled
- **1** of each red and yellow bell peppers, seeded and cut in half
- **3** jalapeño peppers, seeded and cut in half
- ½ butternut squash
- **4 quarts** water
- ¾ **cup** dehydrated sundried tomatoes
- **1 14.5oz can** stewed tomatoes
- **1 tbsp** dried crushed basil
- **1 tbsp** dried crushed rosemary
  freshly ground black pepper, to taste

DIRECTIONS

Combine first four ingredients in a sealable bag or container large enough to hold all vegetables except the squash. Place mushrooms, garlic, carrots, onion, and peppers in marinade. Seal or close container and gently shake and turn to ensure full coverage. Let vegetables marinate for 30 minutes. Grill marinated vegetables on an open fire for approximately 20-30 minutes, turning every 10 minutes. If this is not possible, place vegetables in a roasting pan and bake at 400 degrees for 45 minutes, turning occasionally. Remove seeds from squash and place in a microwaveable dish with 2 tablespoons of water. Cook in microwave long enough to soften, approximately 6-8 minutes on high. Let squash cool enough to touch, and remove skin from squash. Set squash aside. Remove roasting vegetables from heat and let cool enough to touch. Remove as much of the skin from the red and yellow peppers as possible. Add all the vegetables and any unused marinade (or roasting juices from the oven) to a large stockpot. Add all remaining ingredients and bring to a boil, then

reduce heat to simmer and cover. Simmer for one hour and then strain the stock to remove the vegetables. For a delicious thick stock, place strained vegetables into a blender or food processor and puree until smooth. Transfer pureed vegetables back into stockpot, mix well, and continue to simmer another 10 minutes. If you prefer a thin stock, simply discard the strained vegetables. Remove from heat and let covered pot sit for 30 minutes before serving, to allow flavors to combine and stock to cool.

SERVING & LEFTOVER SUGGESTIONS

Serve with a protein source such as chicken breast, or garbanzo or black beans. This also makes a delicious gravy. Enjoy leftovers by adding a few tablespoons per cup of water when cooking rice or other grain that absorbs liquid, or add to your next pasta sauce for a delicious thickening agent.

NUTRITION PER SERVING

106 Calories
3g Protein
2g Fat
21g Carbs
5g Fiber
4g Sugar

gf (use GF soy sauce) *df v*

ROASTED BRUSSELS SPROUTS

SERVES 2-4

I was determined to make the notoriously bland Brussels sprout tasty (but still healthy!) and I was excited to discover what apple cider vinegar and liquid aminos gave them.

INGREDIENTS

½ cup	apple cider vinegar
¼ cup	olive oil
1 tbsp	liquid aminos (or low-sodium soy sauce)
1 tbsp each	garlic, black pepper, no-salt seasoning
25-30	fresh Brussels sprouts, cleaned and halved

DIRECTIONS

Preheat oven to 400 degrees. Combine all ingredients except sprouts in a large baking dish. Add sprouts and toss well. Cover with foil and bake for 45 minutes, removing foil for the last 15 minutes. Serve warm.

SERVING & LEFTOVER SUGGESTIONS

Serve with *Most Loved Chicken* (p. 89) or *Hearty and Healthy Meatloaf* (p. 87) for a delicious and nutritious evening meal. Enjoy leftovers cold on your next salad, or slice Brussels sprouts and mix into a quinoa pilaf with nuts.

NUTRITION PER SERVING

185	Calories
5g	Protein
14g	Fat
15g	Carbs
5g	Fiber
5g	Sugar

gf (use GF soy sauce) *df v*

POWER SALAD

SERVES 2-4

You just might get that promotion, achieve a goal you've been working toward, or save the world after filling up with this mega-nutritious meal!

INGREDIENTS

4 cups fresh spinach, stems removed, chopped
1 cup chopped red cabbage
1 red bell pepper, stem and seeds removed, finely chopped
½ cup fresh mushrooms, finely chopped
½ cup shelled edamame (unsalted)
½ cup black beans, rinsed and drained
4 egg whites, hard-boiled, shells and yolks removed
1 cup salmon, tuna, or skinless chicken breast, pre-cooked
½ cup reduced-fat cottage cheese
Balsamic Vinaigrette (p. 147)

DIRECTIONS

Combine first six ingredients in a large serving bowl; toss well. Arrange egg and meat along top, adding cottage cheese scoop as the final ingredient. Serve with *Balsamic Vinaigrette* (p. 147) and enjoy!

SERVING & LEFTOVER SUGGESTIONS

Stuff leftover salad into a whole wheat pita pocket or add to your morning omelet.

NUTRITION PER SERVING

156 Calories
22g Protein
2g Fat
13g Carbs
4g Fiber
2g Sugar

gf df substitute hummus for cheese   *V* make without fish / meat

SUNSHINE SALAD

SERVES 2-4

This salad takes almost no prep—what an easy way to get your fruits and veggies in together.

INGREDIENTS

4 cups mixed spring greens, chopped
½ cup baby carrots, chopped
1 red bell pepper, stem and seeds removed, finely chopped
½ cup black beans, rinsed and drained
6 ripe strawberries, sliced in half
1 Clementine orange, peeled and sectioned
1 large avocado, cut in half and sliced into bite-sized pieces.

DIRECTIONS

Combine first four ingredients in a large serving bowl, toss well. Arrange fruit and avocado slices on top. Serve with *Hummus Vinaigrette* (p. 155) or *Balsamic Vinaigrette* (p. 147) and enjoy.

SERVING & LEFTOVER SUGGESTIONS

Stuff leftover salad into a whole wheat pita pocket or add to your morning omelet.

NUTRITION PER SERVING

139 Calories
4g Protein
7g Fat
18g Carbs
7g Fiber
4g Sugar

gf df v

SAUTÉED
SPINACH & MUSHROOMS

SERVES 2

This is my all-time favorite vegetable dish to make and eat. It doesn't always make it to a serving dish!

INGREDIENTS

1 tsp	olive oil
1 tbsp	liquid aminos (or low-sodium soy sauce)
¼ cup	apple cider vinegar
1 tbsp	garlic powder
2 tsp	salt-free seasoning
1 tsp	crushed red pepper
4 cups	fresh spinach, stems removed and finely chopped
8 oz	baby bella mushrooms or crimini, thinly sliced
1	large red onion, cut into 1" slices and then quartered

DIRECTIONS

Combine first six ingredients in a large stove top wok or sauté pan. Simmer on low heat for 2-3 minutes. Add all cut vegetables to the pan, stir well, then cover and cook on medium-high heat for 10-15 minutes, stirring frequently to avoid sticking. Remove cover, reduce heat to low, and continue to cook for another 5 minutes. Remove from heat and transfer to a serving bowl.

SERVING & LEFTOVER SUGGESTIONS

Serve with your favorite fish and healthy grain, such as brown rice or quinoa. Load leftovers onto a baked sweet potato for a healthy and delicious meal.

NUTRITION PER SERVING

78	Calories
4g	Protein
3g	Fat
12g	Carbs
3g	Fiber
3g	Sugar

gf (use GF soy sauce) *df v*

GRILLED CHICKEN SALAD
WITH SWEET POTATO

SERVES 2-4

Sweet potatoes on a salad? You'll never miss croutons again.

INGREDIENTS

4 cups fresh spinach, stems removed and chopped
1 cup chopped fresh red cabbage
1 red bell pepper, stem and seeds removed, finely chopped
1 cup sweet potato, pre-cooked and cut into small cubes
2 skinless chicken breast, pre-cooked and cut into small pieces

DIRECTIONS

Combine first three ingredients in a large serving bowl; toss well. Arrange sweet potato and chicken on top of tossed salad. Serve with *Spicy Salsa Dressing* (p. 159) and enjoy!

SERVING & LEFTOVER SUGGESTIONS

Stuff leftover salad into a whole wheat pita pocket or add to your morning omelets.

NUTRITION PER SERVING

140 Calories
16g Protein
2g Fat
15g Carbs
3g Fiber
6g Sugar

gf *df* *v* substitute black beans or hummus for chicken

MASHED CAULIFLOWER

SERVES 2-4

This was an experiment at my brother's house that was inspired after a few glasses of wine. So glad we wrote it down!

INGREDIENTS

- **1 head** cauliflower, cut into small pieces
- **2 tbsp** water
- **1 tbsp** apple cider vinegar
- **1** jalapeño pepper, stem and seeds removed, finely chopped
- **1 tbsp** salt-free mixed seasoning
- **1 tbsp** olive oil
- **2 tsp** garlic powder
- **¼ cup** nutritional yeast

DIRECTIONS

Place cauliflower, water, and vinegar in a bowl. Cover and microwave for 4-6 minutes, until soft. Transfer to a large mixing bowl, add all remaining ingredients, mashing well with a handheld mixer, masher, or food processor until smooth and creamy (think mashed potatoes!). Transfer to a serving bowl and enjoy.

SERVING & LEFTOVER SUGGESTIONS

Add some veggies and shredded chicken, sprinkle some mozzarella cheese and paprika on top, and bake in oven until top is browned.

NUTRITION PER SERVING

- **111** Calories
- **9g** Protein
- **4g** Fat
- **13g** Carbs
- **7g** Fiber
- **0g** Sugar

gf df v

Paprika'd
Sweet Potato Fingers

Serves 4-6

WARNING: These will not last long, they are addictive, and you may not want to share!

INGREDIENTS

2 tbsp garlic powder
2 tbsp paprika
1 tsp chili powder
1 tsp black pepper
4 medium sweet potatoes
2 tbsp olive oil
sea salt to taste

DIRECTIONS

Preheat oven to 425 degrees. Combine all spices in a large freezer bag or other sealable container. Set aside. Cut each potato into 1/3" strips, leaving skin on. Place strips into bag of spices, seal bag, and gently knead or shake until potato strips appear well-coated with spice mixture. Place coated strips in a single layer on a well-oiled cookie sheet. Spray or brush tops with olive oil. Bake for 50-60 minutes, or until strips are well-browned and crisp, but not burned.

SERVING & LEFTOVER SUGGESTIONS

Serve with ketchup or hummus for a fun finger-food appetizer, or as a hearty side with a veggie burger. Slice leftovers into bite-sized pieces and fry with some onions for a great breakfast dish. Or, use the same potato-onion mixture as a great filling for a folded quesadilla.

NUTRITION PER SERVING

108 Calories
2g Protein
5g Fat
16g Carbs
3g Fiber
6g Sugar

gf df v

STUFFED ZUCCHINI

SERVES 4-6

I remember eating lots of stuffed bell peppers growing up, and I wanted to take that idea and make it more healthy while also getting away from never really liking the pepper part and eating just the stuffing. So I browsed through the produce department for a new "vessel" to stuff, and thought I would give the zucchini a try. This is a great solution and everyone enjoys eating every bit of it, including the vessel!

INGREDIENTS

4	medium zucchini squash, stems removed and sliced lengthwise
1 tsp	olive oil
1 tbsp	crushed garlic
6 oz	portabella mushrooms, finely chopped
1	red bell pepper, stem and seeds removed, finely chopped
½	large red onion, finely chopped
¼ cup	pinon nuts
¼ cup	balsamic vinegar
¼ cup	fresh basil, finely chopped
3 oz	reduced-fat feta cheese
	freshly ground black pepper, to taste

DIRECTIONS

Leave skin on zucchini halves, and scoop out all but ¼ inch of inner squash. Put removed parts aside. Sauté garlic, mushroom, bell pepper, onion, nuts, pepper, and balsamic vinegar in olive oil. Add removed inner squash and sauté for 10-15 minutes until lightly browned. Transfer cooked vegetable mixture to a large mixing bowl and fold in chopped basil. Set aside. Tear 6 pieces of aluminum foil large enough to wrap zucchini halves in. Set these out so they are ready for you to wrap as you stuff the zucchini. With a spoon, generously overfill each zucchini half with the stuffing and use your hands to mold the overflowing stuffing for each half. Place the stuffed zucchini in the center of a sheet of foil and loosely wrap until completely sealed. Repeat this for each zucchini half. Place foil packages on an open grill or an oven preheated at 375 degrees, for 5-10 minutes on each side. remove foil packages from heat source and let them cool 5 minutes before unwrapping and placing on a serving platter.

SERVING & LEFTOVER SUGGESTIONS

Chop up cold leftovers and add to your lunch salad, or fold into a quesadilla.

NUTRITION PER SERVING

97 Calories
4g Protein
7g Fat
8g Carbs
3g Fiber
3g Sugar

gf df substitute hummus for cheese *v*

Garden Salad
with Avocado & Sunflower Seeds

Serves 2-4

One of my favorite ways to get lots of healthy fats and fiber into my day, and not to mention delicious!

INGREDIENTS

4 cups fresh spinach, stems removed and chopped
1 cup chopped fresh red cabbage
4 baby bella mushrooms, sliced
1 bell pepper—orange or yellow, stem and seeds removed, chopped
10 small grape tomatoes, cut in half lengthwise
1 large avocado, cut in half and sliced into bite-sized pieces
¼ cup raw, unsalted sunflower seeds

DIRECTIONS

Combine first three ingredients in a large serving bowl, toss well. Arrange tomatoes and avocado on top. Sprinkle with sunflower seeds. Serve with *Hummus Vinaigrette* (p. 155) and enjoy.

SERVING & LEFTOVER SUGGESTIONS

Stuff leftover salad into a whole wheat pita pocket or add to your morning omelet.

NUTRITION PER SERVING

147 Calories
4g Protein
11g Fat
12g Carbs
5g Fiber
2g Sugar

gf df v

GRILLED AVOCADO

MAKES 6 HALVES

This is a showstopper, trust me! You can even start with slightly under-ripe avocados and have soft delicious flesh to eat after they come off the grill.

INGREDIENTS

3 avocados, cut in half, seed removed
1 tbsp olive oil
1 tsp garlic powder

DIRECTIONS

Mix olive oil and garlic in a small bowl. Lay avocado halves on a platter, skin side down, and liberally brush each half with garlic and olive oil mixture. Place avocados skin side down on the grill and cook on a medium flame for 5 minutes. Turn each half and grill for another 5 minutes. Remove from heat and serve while warm.

SERVING & LEFTOVER SUGGESTIONS

Serve as a delicious and healthy topping on your grilled fish, chicken, or beef. Use leftovers on your next salad or as the base for guacamole.

NUTRITION PER SERVING

164 Calories
2g Protein
16g Fat
8g Carbs
6g Fiber
0g Sugar

gf df v

SAVORY QUINOA PILAF

SERVES 4-6

This is a great way to introduce the family to "keen-wa,"
the super-healthy gluten-free grain.

INGREDIENTS

1 tsp	olive oil
½	large red onion, finely chopped
6 oz	baby portabella mushrooms, finely chopped
½ cup	sliced almonds
3 cups	fresh spinach, chopped
1 tbsp	minced garlic
2 tsp	chili powder
2 tbsp	balsamic vinegar
1	can black beans, drained and rinsed well
1 5.5oz can	low-sodium V-8 juice
3 cups	water
2 cups	quinoa
½ cup	fresh cilantro, finely chopped
	freshly ground black pepper, to taste

DIRECTIONS

Heat oil in a large frying pan and sauté onion, mushrooms, and almonds 5-7 minutes until lightly browned. Add spinach, garlic, pepper, chili powder, balsamic vinegar, and black beans; sauté another 5 minutes. Add V-8 juice, water, and quinoa. Bring contents to a boil, stir well, reduce heat, and cover. Let contents simmer, covered, for another 15-20 minutes or until most of the liquid is absorbed. Remove cover and add fresh cilantro, mixing one final time before serving.

SERVING & LEFTOVER SUGGESTIONS

Serve with your favorite grilled chicken or fish. Enjoy leftovers cold as a great alternative to pasta salad.

NUTRITION PER SERVING

241 Calories
11g Protein
7g Fat
36g Carbs
8g Fiber
2g Sugar

gf df v

SPINACH SALAD
WITH FRUIT & NUTS

SERVES 4-6

I usually pile lots of veggies in my salads, but when I have dinner parties, I like to use the salad as a supporting role, not the lead. So I came up with this simple combination of elegant ingredients that set the stage nicely for whatever the next course is.

INGREDIENTS

4 cups fresh spinach leaves, stems removed and chopped
2 thin slices of red onion, rings separated and quartered
1 chilled Asian pear or Granny Smith apple, peeled, cored, and sliced thin
1 oz rumbled reduced-fat feta cheese
½ cup spiced walnuts, prepared ahead of time*

DIRECTIONS

Toss all ingredients together in a large salad serving bowl and cover. Chill in refrigerator for 1 hour prior to serving. Remove cover and serve with balsamic-based dressing.

*Spiced Walnuts: Preheat oven to 375 degrees. Mix nuts in a bowl with 1 tbsp each of cinnamon and warmed honey. Place in a single layer on a lightly oiled cookie sheet and bake for 15 minutes.

SERVING & LEFTOVER SUGGESTIONS

Add more crumbled feta cheese and a drizzle of dressing, and stuff pita pocket halves, for a delicious lunch.

NUTRITION PER SERVING

88 Calories
3g Protein
7g Fat
5g Carbs
2g Fiber
2g Sugar

gf *df* substitute tofu for cheese *v*

VEGGIE GRILL

SERVES 3

*This has been voted a #1 recipe by my house guests and family.
We never get tired of it and it makes us all say "mmm!"*

INGREDIENTS

6 mushrooms, stems intact
1 red onion, peeled and quartered
1 of each red, yellow, and orange bell peppers, sliced in half, stem and seeds removed
2 hearts of romaine, sliced in half lengthwise
10 asparagus spears

DIRECTIONS

Combine all ingredients in a sealable plastic bag or container. Make *Fresh Vegetable Marinade* (p. 143) and pour over vegetables, letting it marinate for at least 30 minutes. Grill veggies over medium heat, turning once or twice to desired doneness.

SERVING & LEFTOVER SUGGESTIONS

Serve with *Grilled Avocado* (p. 59). Chop leftovers up for a morning omelet.

NUTRITION PER SERVING

95 Calories
6g Protein
1g Fat
20g Carbs
5g Fiber
1g Sugar

gf df v

Evening Meals

Angel Hair Pasta
with Cannelinis & Greens

SERVES 4

What a great way to enjoy Italian food with beans and greens that are good for you!

INGREDIENTS

1 14oz box	whole wheat angel hair pasta
3 cups	fresh arugula or chopped fresh spinach
1 cup	frozen peas, thawed and rinsed in warm water
4 cups	*Spicy Marinara Sauce* (p. 157), heated
1 14.5oz can	cannellini beans, rinsed and drained
1 4oz can	mild green chiles
¼ cup	freshly grated parmesan cheese

DIRECTIONS

Cook pasta according to directions. Strain and transfer to a large serving bowl. Evenly spread the arugula and peas over the top of the pasta. Next, ladle all of the sauce over the pasta, arugula, and peas. This will cause the arugula to wilt. Evenly distribute the beans and chiles over the sauce. Top with parmesan cheese and serve immediately.

SERVING & LEFTOVER SUGGESTIONS

Serve with a fresh spinach salad. Mix contents well before storing leftovers. Reheat for a delicious lunch or dinner.

NUTRITION PER SERVING

611	Calories
29g	Protein
10g	Fat
110g	Carbs
23g	Fiber
2g	Sugar

df make without cheese *v*

Baked Chicken & Sweet Potato
Casserole

Serves 2-4

I love to Jen-ify comfort foods, so this was my healthy spin on traditional shepherd's pie. It is so hearty and full of warmth, and reminds me of cold winter days as a little girl.

INGREDIENTS

3	large sweet potatoes, cut into quarters (leave skin on, it's nutritious!)
2 cups	fat-free cottage cheese
1 cup	salsa
2	chicken breasts, pre-cooked, pulled into bite-sized shreds
1 cup	mixed vegetables (frozen, fresh, or leftovers work great!)
⅓ cup	sliced almonds

DIRECTIONS

Preheat oven to 375 degrees. Microwave sweet potatoes until soft, approximately 7 minutes. Remove cooked potatoes and slice open to allow them to cool enough to handle. Add cottage cheese and salsa to a large bowl and mash with a fork to a fairly smooth consistency. Add chicken and vegetables, mixing all ingredients well. Transfer contents to a well-oiled baking dish. Smooth out and flatten top with a spatula. Sprinkle sliced almonds over top. Cover with foil and bake for 45 minutes, removing the foil for the last 10 minutes.

NUTRITION PER SERVING

338	Calories
44g	Protein
5g	Fat
29g	Carbs
5g	Fiber
13g	Sugar

BAKED STUFFED SHELLS
WITH PINONS

SERVES 4-6

This is a holiday tradition in my house, and we often experiment with different stuffings.

INGREDIENTS

1 box	jumbo pasta shells
1 tsp	olive oil
1 tbsp	finely chopped green onion
1 tbsp	minced garlic
½ cup	pinon nuts
2 cups	fresh spinach, finely chopped
2 cups	low-fat cottage cheese
1 cup	parmesan cheese, finely shredded
2 tbsp	fresh basil, finely chopped
1 tbsp	paprika
2 tsp	freshly ground black pepper
½ cup	shredded part-skim mozzarella cheese

DIRECTIONS

Preheat oven to 375 degrees. Cook pasta shells according to instructions, being careful not to overcook. Strain and rinse cooked shells in cool water. Put aside for later use. Heat oil in sauté pan. Add onion, garlic, and nuts. Sauté on high heat for 5-7 minutes, adding spinach for the last 2 minutes. Transfer cooked mixture to a large mixing bowl and let cool to room temperature. Add cottage cheese, parmesan cheese, basil, paprika, and pepper to contents of the bowl. Mix well and set aside for stuffing. Lightly oil the bottom and sides of a large baking dish. Fill each shell with a generous portion of stuffing and place stuffed side up in the baking dish. Repeat until all stuffing or shells are used. Sprinkle tops of shells with mozzarella cheese and loosely cover with aluminum foil. Bake for 25 minutes. Remove foil and bake an additional 5 minutes. Remove from oven and serve with your favorite pasta sauce (p. 157 for ideas).

SERVING & LEFTOVER SUGGESTIONS

Serve one or two leftover shells as a side dish with a large salad or your favorite meat.

NUTRITION PER SERVING

464 Calories
30g Protein
18g Fat
47g Carbs
2g Fiber
3g Sugar

V

Four Bean Cabin Chili

Serves 6-8

I created this winter favorite one year while visiting a friend's cabin in the pines of northern Arizona. We enjoyed it all day long... even for breakfast the next day!

INGREDIENTS

3 cups	tomato puree
1 20oz can	whole, peeled plum tomatoes
3 tbsp	garlic powder
3 tbsp	chili powder
1 tbsp	hot taco seasoning
2 tbsp	ground cumin
1 tbsp	ground Mexican oregano
1 tbsp	dried basil
2	vegetable bouillon cubes
1 tbsp	olive oil
1	large red onion, peeled
2	large carrots, tops removed, peeled
1	red bell pepper, stems and seeds removed
1 tbsp	minced garlic
¼ cup	balsamic vinegar
1 cup	dry lentils, rinsed and soaked for 1-2 hours
1 30oz can	chili beans, rinsed
1 15oz can	red kidney beans, rinsed
1 15oz can	black beans, rinsed
1 ½ cup	frozen sweet petite corn, thawed and drained well
1 8oz can	green chiles, diced
1 cup	salsa verde
handful	fresh cilantro, chopped

DIRECTIONS

In a large crock pot, combine the following ingredients: tomato puree, plum tomatoes, garlic powder, pepper, chili powder, taco seasoning, cumin, oregano, basil, and vegetable bouillon. Set to highest temperature. As you add ingredients, stir occasionally to prevent sticking/burning; total cooking time on high should be between 1-2 hours.

Heat oil in a large pan. Chop onion and red bell pepper into small pieces. Cut carrots lengthwise into quarters, and chop into small pieces. Sauté the chopped vegetables, adding the minced garlic and balsamic vinegar. Sauté until onions and peppers are soft and browned. Carrots will still be firm—these will soften in the crock pot.

75

Add sautéed vegetables to crock pot. Add soaked and cleaned lentils to a pot of boiling water; cook until only slightly tender, approximately 15-25 minutes. Drain and add to crock pot. After crock pot has been cooking on high for 1-2 hours, lower setting to lowest, a slow simmer. Now add all remaining ingredients except cilantro and mix to combine. Let the chili simmer for 2-3 hours. After simmering is complete, let chili sit, covered, for another half hour before serving. Top each individual serving with some chopped fresh cilantro.

SERVING & LEFTOVER SUGGESTIONS

Use as a topping on a baked sweet potato, or puree and pour over pasta for a high-protein, tasty, tomato-based sauce alternative.

NUTRITION PER SERVING

434 Calories
25g Protein
4g Fat
81g Carbs
25g Fiber
6g Sugar

gf df v

BODY-LOVING BAKED TOFU

SERVES 4

This is the un-tofu recipe that you have been looking for.

INGREDIENTS

1 package extra-firm tofu, pressed (for maximum flavor)
1 tbsp Dijon mustard
1 tbsp almond butter
1 tbsp sesame seed oil
2 tsp chili paste
2 tsp apple cider vinegar
1 tsp each dried basil, garlic, and black pepper

DIRECTIONS

Preheat oven to 400 degrees. Combine all ingredients except tofu in a large mixing bowl. Cut pressed tofu into small cubes and add to marinade in bowl. Gently mix to ensure even coverage, then transfer all contents of bowl into a well-oiled baking dish (I recommend non-stick or disposable aluminum pans for easier clean up). Bake uncovered for 30 minutes, then turn the cubes over and bake another 15 minutes. Remove from oven and transfer to serving bowl.

SERVING & LEFTOVER SUGGESTIONS

These little guys taste even better cold the next day, and are super easy to pop in your mouth wherever your adventures take you. You can use this as a meat substitute in just about any meal, and you may want to double up on the batch since you are firing up the oven anyway—enjoy!

NUTRITION PER SERVING

164 Calories
12g Protein
13g Fat
3g Carbs
1g Fiber
1g Sugar

gf df v

Bok Choy, Mushroom, & Broccoli
Stir-Fry

Serves 4

I remember the first time I bought bok choy. I wanted to try it, but had no idea how to use it. I have since discovered the fun 2-step approach to bok choy: cook the stalks to soften (like you would with celery) and simply wilt the greens (like spinach). It's like two veggies in one!

INGREDIENTS

1 tsp	sesame seed oil
1 tbsp	liquid aminos (or low-sodium soy sauce)
1 tbsp	teriyaki sauce
1 tbsp	balsamic vinegar
1 tbsp	lemon juice
1 tbsp	garlic powder
1 head	bok choy
8 oz	baby bella mushrooms or crimini, quartered
1 head	broccoli, florets cut into bite-sized pieces
1	large red onion, cut into 1" slices and then quartered
2	medium green bell peppers, stem and seeds removed, cut lengthwise into 1" strips

DIRECTIONS

To prepare bok choy for cooking, remove stems from leaves. Shred or slice leaves into long strips and set aside. Slice stems into 1" pieces. Combine first six ingredients in a large stovetop wok or paella pan. Simmer on low heat for 2-3 minutes. Add all cut vegetables to the pan except bok choy leaves. Stir well, then cover and cook on medium-high heat for 10-15 minutes, stirring frequently to avoid sticking. Add bok choy leaves, reduce heat to low, and continue to cook, covered, for another 10 minutes. Remove from heat and transfer to a serving bowl along with your favorite healthy grain, such as brown rice or quinoa.

SERVING & LEFTOVER SUGGESTIONS

Load onto a baked potato for a healthy and delicious meal.

NUTRITION PER SERVING

98 Calories
8g Protein
2g Fat
17g Carbs
6g Fiber
3g Sugar

gf (use GF soy sauce and teriyaki) *df* *v*

"Bounty Bowl"

Serves 1

I love this meal for one that is also an all-in-one meal!

INGREDIENTS

1	small sweet potato, cut into bite-sized pieces, with skin on
½ cup	fat-free cottage cheese
½ cup	salsa (chunky and spicy works best in this dish)
1	pre-cooked skinless chicken breast, pulled into bite-sized shreds

DIRECTIONS

Place sweet potato chunks in a bowl with a splash of water. Cover and microwave for 3-4 minutes. Add remaining ingredients to bowl, toss for even coverage, and enjoy!

NUTRITION PER SERVING

347 Calories
39g Protein
3g Fat
42g Carbs
5g Fiber
5g Sugar

HEALTHY FISH TACOS

SERVES 2

Easy and delicious? Oh yeah! This dish is fun to eat and reminds me of a great beach vacation!

INGREDIENTS

8 oz	tilapia filets, cut into small bite-sized pieces
1 tsp	olive oil
2 tbsp	lemon juice
1 tsp	garlic powder
4	small corn tortillas
2 cups	red cabbage, shredded or finely chopped
1 cup	fresh spinach, finely chopped
2	celery stalks, finely chopped
½ cup	fresh cilantro, finely chopped

DIRECTIONS

Saute first four ingredients over medium heat, 5-10 minutes, until fish is nicely browned. Lay tortillas on flat surface, and evenly distribute all ingredients to build tacos. Finish each taco with a drizzle of your favorite dressing, fold, and enjoy!

SERVING & LEFTOVER SUGGESTIONS

Prepare *Spicy Fish Taco Sauce* (p. 153) or *Fresh Fish Taco Sauce* (p. 151) for a delicious and healthy alternative to cream-based sauces.

NUTRITION PER SERVING

277	Calories
28g	Protein
6g	Fat
31g	Carbs
7g	Fiber
1g	Sugar

gf df

HEALTHY BEEF & VEGETABLE
KABOBS

SERVES 4

This was created during my maiden voyage with the largest outdoor grill I have ever owned – and it was filled with healthy morsels of grilled heaven that was shared with a house full of friends.

INGREDIENTS

16 oz lean sirloin steak, cut into cubes
2 red onions, peeled and cut into large chunks
3 bell peppers (red, yellow, and orange), stem and seeds removed, cut into large pieces
16 baby bella mushrooms, stems intact

Beef Marinade:
¼ cup apple cider vinegar
1 tbsp liquid aminos (or low-sodium soy sauce)
1 5.5oz can low-sodium V-8
1 tbsp Dijon mustard
1 tbsp garlic powder
1 tbsp dried oregano
1 tbsp black pepper

Vegetable Marinade:
2 tbsp olive oil
2 tbsp apple cider vinegar
2 tsp liquid aminos (or low-sodium soy sauce)
1 tsp crushed garlic
1 tsp black pepper

DIRECTIONS

Combine all beef marinade ingredients in a sealable container large enough to also hold meat. Add beef cubes and allow to marinate for 2 hours. Combine all vegetable marinade ingredients in a sealable container large enough to also hold vegetables. Add cut vegetables and allow to marinate for 1-2 hours. Skewer all marinated ingredients and grill on a medium flame for 10 minutes, turning frequently and using remaining vegetable marinade halfway through the cook time.

SERVING & LEFTOVER SUGGESTIONS

Serve with *Paprika'd Sweet Potato Fingers* (p. 53) and *Spinach Salad with Fruit & Nuts* (p. 63) on the side. Finely chop leftovers and make a breakfast burrito or omelet for breakfast.

NUTRITION PER SERVING

281 Calories
41g Protein
9g Fat
8g Carbs
1g Fiber
4g Sugar

gf (use GF soy sauce) *df*

HEARTY & HEALTHY MEATLOAF

SERVES 4-6

This dish delivers your protein (sirloin, turkey, eggs), complex carbs and fiber (oats, apple), and healthy fat (walnuts, flaxseed) all in one hearty bundle!

INGREDIENTS

1 cup	oats
2 tbsp	ground flaxseed meal
3	egg whites
1	apple, cored and diced (leave skin on)
½ cup	walnuts, broken into small pieces
½ cup	chopped veggies (any fresh, leftover, or frozen mix will do)
½ cup	tomato sauce
1 tbsp each	dried basil, parsley, ground chili powder, black pepper, dried garlic
1 lb	ground sirloin
1 lb	lean ground turkey

DIRECTIONS

Preheat oven to 375 degrees. Mix all ingredients, except for half the tomato sauce, which you can put aside for later. Form mixture into a long loaf (more flat and long than short and thick) in a lightly oiled baking dish. Spread remaining tomato sauce on top of loaf, cover with foil, and bake for 60 minutes, removing the foil for the final 20 minutes. Check center of meatloaf to ensure fully cooked (should not be pink) and remove from oven, allowing to cool slightly before serving.

SERVING & LEFTOVER SUGGESTIONS

This makes amazingly easy and delicious road food. Slice it into individual servings, refrigerate it, and enjoy on the go as finger food. Leftovers make great sandwiches – add a little tomato sauce and mozzarella cheese and enjoy.

NUTRITION PER SERVING

386 Calories
42g Protein
16g Fat
19g Carbs
4g Fiber
6g Sugar

gf df

MOST-LOVED CHICKEN

SERVES 4-6

Everyone loves this Most-Loved Chicken—it's a tasty way to eat clean.

INGREDIENTS

4-6	large boneless, skinless chicken breasts
1 5.5oz can	low-sodium V-8
½ cup	apple cider vinegar
2 tbsp	Dijon mustard
¼ cup	water
¼ cup	dried onion flakes
2 tbsp	garlic powder
1 tbsp	paprika
1 tbsp	dried basil

DIRECTIONS

Preheat oven to 425 degrees. Combine all ingredients to yield enough marinade for 4-6 large chicken breasts. Place marinade and chicken breasts in a large glass baking dish, cover with foil, and marinate in the refrigerator for 2-4 hours. Bake chicken breasts for 40 minutes; remove foil, turn chicken breasts, and bake, uncovered, for another 15 minutes. Remove chicken from oven and cool to desired warmth before serving.

SERVING & LEFTOVER SUGGESTIONS

Serve with *Paprika'd Sweet Potato Fingers* (p. 53) and a nice green salad. Leftovers are delicious as a shredded topping to salad, stuffing to a healthy pita sandwich or quesadilla, or as the star in rice pilaf.

NUTRITION PER SERVING

112	Calories
20g	Protein
2g	Fat
2g	Carbs
0g	Fiber
2g	Sugar

gf df

One-Pan
Chicken Stir-Fry with Quinoa

Serves 4

I created this one-pan wonder for an appearance on a TV show that was geared towards busy moms. I remember how surprised the host was to see me add uncooked quinoa right in the same pan!

INGREDIENTS

1 tbsp	olive oil
1 tbsp	liquid aminos (or low-sodium soy sauce)
1 tbsp	granulated garlic
2	large boneless, skinless chicken breasts cut into small strips
1 tbsp	apple cider vinegar (or lemon juice)
1 tbsp	teriyaki sauce
1 tbsp	black pepper
1 head	bok choy, chopped leaves and stems
8 oz	baby bella mushrooms, sliced
1	large red onion, cut into 1" slices and then quartered
2	medium green bell peppers, stem and seeds removed, cut lengthwise into 1" strips
1 cup	quinoa
2 cups	water
1 small can	low-sodium V-8 juice
1 tbsp	dried cilantro
¼ cup	sliced almonds

DIRECTIONS

Sauté the first 4 ingredients in a large, deep pan for 6-10 minutes on high heat, browning well. Add the next 7 ingredients and sauté on high heat for 10 minutes. Add the next 4 ingredients and bring to a boil. Cover and reduce heat to simmer, cooking another 10-15 minutes until quinoa is cooked to desired softness. Mix almonds into the finished dish and enjoy!

SERVING & LEFTOVER SUGGESTIONS

Use leftovers as a stuffing in a quesadilla or lunch wrap.

NUTRITION PER SERVING

373 Calories
27g Protein
11g Fat
46g Carbs
7g Fiber
4g Sugar

gf (use GF soy sauce) *df*

SPAGHETTI SQUASH ITALIANO

SERVES 2

Such a fun and healthy alternative to pasta—you will love it!

INGREDIENTS

1	spaghetti squash
1 cup	fresh baby spinach, stems removed
1 cup	fat-free cottage cheese
½ cup	frozen peas, thawed and rinsed
4 cups	all-natural pasta sauce
½ cup	parmesan cheese, freshly grated

DIRECTIONS

Cut spaghetti squash in half and place cut side down in a glass baking dish, with ¼ inch of water in the bottom of the dish. Microwave on high for 8-10 minutes, or until squash is easily removed with a fork. Remove seeds, and then use a fork to "shred" squash out of skin. Remove all the squash in this fashion and place in a large serving bowl. Evenly spread spinach over top of warm spaghetti squash, followed by sauce. Add cottage cheese and peas. Sprinkle parmesan cheese over entire dish and serve immediately.

SERVING & LEFTOVER SUGGESTIONS

Mix well before storing leftovers. Reheat for a delicious lunch or dinner, or chop and add as a hearty topping to a green salad.

NUTRITION PER SERVING

495	Calories
35g	Protein
14g	Fat
62g	Carbs
10g	Fiber
33g	Sugar

gf v

STUFFED ACORN SQUASH

SERVES 2

I was never a huge squash fan, but quickly became one once I realized it could be a healthy vessel to hold a bounty of other things. I had fun experimenting with different stuffings and really loved this warm and hearty combination.

INGREDIENTS

1	large acorn squash
½ cup	water
1 tbsp	olive oil
5-7	white mushrooms, finely chopped
½	red bell pepper, stem and seeds removed, finely chopped
¼	red onion, finely chopped
½ cup	pinons
1 cup	balsamic vinegar
1 tbsp	crushed garlic
2 tsp	freshly ground black pepper
½ can	garbanzo beans, rinsed and drained
1 tsp	paprika
2 tbsp	fresh basil, stems removed and chopped
1 tsp	ground cumin
1 tsp	crushed rosemary
½ cup	crushed whole wheat crackers or stale wheat bread
¾ cup	tomato sauce
½ cup	part-skim mozzarella cheese, shredded

DIRECTIONS

Preheat oven to 350 degrees. Cut squash in half and remove seeds. Cut enough of ends off to allow squash halves to sit flat in dish. Pour water in a baking dish and place squash halves cut side up in the water. Cover dish with aluminum foil and bake for 25 minutes. While squash is cooking, prepare the stuffing. Heat olive oil in sauté pan. Add the chopped mushrooms, bell peppers, onion, and nuts. Saute on high heat for 5-7 minutes, stirring frequently. Add balsamic vinegar, garlic, black pepper, and garbanzo beans and continue to sauté for 5 more minutes. Transfer cooked mixture, including any remaining liquid, into a large mixing bowl. Add all remaining ingredients except cheese and 4 tablespoons of the tomato sauce. Mix well and put aside. Remove cooked squash from oven and drain water out of pan.

Generously stuff each half of squash evenly, building up to a rounded mound in the middle of each. (Any unused stuffing may be placed in the bottom of the dish after applying some oil to prevent sticking.) Top each

mound with half of the shredded cheese and half of the reserved tomato sauce. Bake stuffed squash halves, uncovered, at 350 for 10 minutes. Switch oven to broil for an additional 10 minutes, ensuring the tops of the stuffed squash are not too close to the broiler. Remove squash from oven, transfer to a serving platter, and serve hot.

SERVING & LEFTOVER SUGGESTIONS

Remove leftovers from skin and serve over pasta with some marinara sauce.

NUTRITION PER SERVING

457 Calories
16g Protein
22g Fat
51g Carbs
7g Fiber
3g Sugar

gf substitute quinoa for crackers *v*

Party Foods
& Snacks

Baked Cheese Heaven

Serves 4-6

This is a party favorite that never lasts long!

INGREDIENTS

12 oz reduced-fat cream cheese, softened
¾ cup reduced-fat feta cheese, crumbled
¾ cup fat-free plain Greek yogurt
3 tbsp Dijon mustard
2 tbsp minced garlic
1 tsp dried herbs (basil, oregano, or rosemary)
1 tsp paprika
¼ cup grated parmesan cheese
freshly ground black pepper, to taste

DIRECTIONS

Preheat oven to 425 degrees. Combine all ingredients except parmesan and paprika in a large mixing bowl and mix well. Coat shallow baking dish with nonstick spray and evenly spread mixture. Sprinkle parmesan and paprika on top and cover loosely with aluminum foil. Bake for 20 minutes; remove foil and bake an additional 5 minutes or until top is slightly browned. Let cool 10 minutes before serving.

SERVING & LEFTOVER SUGGESTIONS

Use leftovers as stuffing in a quesadilla or lunch wrap.

NUTRITION PER SERVING

254 Calories
19g Protein
18g Fat
5g Carbs
0g Fiber
1g Sugar

Feta & Portabella Pizza

Makes 1 pizza

I remember teaching a healthy foodie club how to make healthy pizza, and this was one of the pizzas I took them through step-by-step. Being lovers of a good crust, they were thrilled to learn my techniques to avoid soggy crust syndrome.

INGREDIENTS

1 tsp	olive oil
1 tbsp	minced garlic
1	large portabella mushroom, finely chopped
½	red onion, sliced very thin and then quartered
2 tbsp	balsamic vinegar
1 batch	whole wheat pizza dough* and flour to work dough with
1 cup	*Fresh and Easy Pizza Sauce*** (p. 141)
1 tbsp	fresh basil, chopped
2 cups	shredded mozzarella cheese
4 oz	feta cheese, crumbled
	freshly ground black pepper, to taste

DIRECTIONS

Preheat oven and pizza stone according to directions of stone you are using. Heat oil in a skillet, mixing in garlic and pepper. Sauté mushroom and onion in oil until softened and slightly browned, adding balsamic vinegar for last few minutes. Set aside. Roll out dough, using flour on surface to avoid sticking. Prepare pizza board according to baking stone instructions. Place dough on board. Roll ends up to create a crust. Ladle sauce evenly onto prepared dough, and follow with basil, mushrooms, onions and both cheeses. Cook according to baking stone instructions, and serve warm.

*Many great ready-to-roll pizza dough options exist in the refrigerated section of your grocery store. No need to make dough from scratch!
**Store-bought pizza or pasta sauce can be spiced up to meet your personal taste; alternatively, this is a great use for any leftover homemade sauce—just add a little canned tomato sauce to thin out if needed.

SERVING & LEFTOVER SUGGESTIONS

There won't be leftovers!

NUTRITION PER SERVING

365 Calories
20g Protein
16g Fat
35g Carbs
6g Fiber
3g Sugar

v

SMOKY VEGETABLE & PIÑON PIZZA

MAKES 1 PIZZA

This was created especially for a healthy pizza demonstration I did for a foodie club in Scottsdale. The smoked cheese gives this a unique flavor that is balanced by the mild flavor of the pine nuts.

INGREDIENTS

1 tbsp olive oil
1 tbsp fresh garlic, minced
1 tbsp crushed rosemary
2 cups fresh spinach, finely chopped
4 oz baby bella mushrooms, finely chopped
½ each red, yellow, and orange bell peppers, stem and seeds removed, sliced very thin and cut in half
½ red onion, sliced very thin and quartered
2 tbsp pinons (pine nuts)
2 tbsp balsamic vinegar
1 batch whole wheat pizza dough* and flour to work dough with
1 cup *Fresh and Easy Pizza Sauce*** (p. 141)
1 tbsp fresh basil, chopped
2 cups shredded smoked mozzarella cheese
freshly ground black pepper, to taste

DIRECTIONS

Preheat oven and pizza stone according to directions of stone you are using. Heat oil in a skillet, mixing in garlic, rosemary, and pepper. Saute vegetables and nuts in oil until slightly browned, adding balsamic vinegar for last few minutes. Set aside. Roll out dough, using flour on surface to avoid sticking. Prepare pizza board according to baking stone instructions. Place dough on board. Roll ends up to create a crust. Ladle sauce evenly onto prepared dough, and follow with cheese, then vegetable mix. Cook according to baking stone instructions, and garnish with basil before serving.

*Many great ready-to-roll pizza dough options exist in the refrigerated section of your grocery store. No need to make dough from scratch!
**Store-bought pizza or pasta sauce can be spiced up to meet your personal taste; alternatively, this is a great use for any leftover homemade sauce—just add a little canned tomato sauce to thin out if needed.

SERVING & LEFTOVER SUGGESTIONS

There won't be leftovers!

NUTRITION PER SERVING

361 Calories
22g Protein
15g Fat
32g Carbs
6g Fiber
3g Sugar

V

TIRAMISU ANGELS

SERVES 8

I remember being a little girl and my Nana making her version of this classic Italian dessert. I loved it so much and felt like a big girl because they let me have a small piece even though it had an adult beverage in the cake! I created this lower-calorie version that has every bit of flavor and celebration as the ones from my childhood.

INGREDIENTS

¼ cup	stevia sugar substitute (or equivalent of 1 ¼ cup sugar)
8 oz	reduced-fat cream cheese
1 ½ cups	fat-free whipped topping, thawed
¼ cup	water
3	egg whites
½ cup	espresso, cooled
4 tbsp	dark spiced rum
1	angel food cake
3 tbsp	fat-free whipped topping, thawed
1 tbsp	unsweetened cocoa
2 tsp	ground cinnamon
1 tbsp	ground nutmeg

DIRECTIONS

Combine half of the sugar substitute with the cream cheese in bowl and beat at high speed until well-blended. Gently fold 1 cup of whipped topping into cheese mixture; do not overmix. Combine the remaining sugar substitute with water and egg whites in a separate bowl that has been warmed (to do this, run empty bowl under warm to hot water and dry thoroughly). Gently stir 1/4 of egg white mixture into cheese mixture; gently fold in remaining egg mixture. In another small bowl, combine espresso and rum; stir well. Slice angel food cake horizontally into three sections (use a bread knife to prevent tearing). Place one slice in the bottom of a round glass trifle bowl. If bowl is narrowest at the bottom, be sure to start with the narrowest or top slice of the angel food cake, graduating to wider slices as you fill up the bowl. Use 1 tbsp of whipped topping to fill center hole of angel food cake. Drizzle 1/3 of espresso mixture over angel food slice, then spread 1/3 of cheese mixture over slice as well. Repeat process with remaining 2 angel food slices, whipped topping to fill hole, espresso mixture, and cheese mixture. Garnish with sprinkled cocoa, cinnamon, and nutmeg. Place one toothpick in each corner and center of tiramisu to prevent plastic wrap from sticking to whipped topping, then cover with plastic wrap and refrigerate for 2 hours; serve immediately.

SERVING & LEFTOVER SUGGESTIONS

Serve cold right out of the refrigerator for best consistency. This is an excellent dessert for any Italian dinner because it is so light and airy.

NUTRITION PER SERVING

- **281** Calories
- **41g** Protein
- **9g** Fat
- **8g** Carbs
- **1g** Fiber
- **4g** Sugar

V

ZESTY PITA CHIPS

SERVES 4

*This is one of my entertaining staples and it will likely become one of yours!
Kids love these too!*

INGREDIENTS

4 whole pita bread rounds, whole wheat
1 tsp olive oil, preferably extra virgin
1 tsp granulated garlic
1 tsp onion powder
1 tsp chili powder
1 tsp paprika
1 tsp crushed basil
1 tsp ground cumin
freshly ground black pepper, to taste

DIRECTIONS

Preheat oven to a high broil. Combine all dry spices in a bowl; set aside.
Slice pita rounds into quarters. Gently separate each quarter into two
pieces. Arrange in a single later on a nonstick baking sheet. Place
triangles close together, leaving no space between (slightly overlapping
if necessary). Spray or brush olive oil evenly over the tops of the triangles.
Evenly sprinkle spice mixture over all triangles. Broil for 3-5 minutes, until
triangles are well toasted. Remove from oven immediately. Remove
triangles from baking sheet to cool, keeping toasted side up. After cooled,
arrange in layers around the perimeter of a large, flat serving platter,
leaving the center open for a bowl of your favorite relish or dip.

SERVING & LEFTOVER SUGGESTIONS

Serve with *Four Pepper & Mango Pico de Gallo* (p. 139). Top leftovers with
low-fat cottage cheese and your favorite salsa for a high energy snack.

NUTRITION PER SERVING

180 Calories
6g Protein
3g Fat
35g Carbs
5g Fiber
0g Sugar

df v

ALMOND BUTTER & FRUIT
PINWHEELS

MAKES 6

These pinwheels taste like candy! This is a great healthy fix for a sweet tooth or a midday energy booster, while helping your circulatory system perform at its best. Watch out, though, the kids will want you to share.

INGREDIENTS

1 whole wheat tortilla
3 tbsp almond butter
1 CocoaVia packet, any fruit flavor*
½ pear, finely chopped

DIRECTIONS

Lay tortilla flat and evenly cover with almond butter. Sprinkle CocoaVia over almond butter, and finish with a layer of chopped pear. Tightly roll tortilla into a long tube and slice ends off. Slice into six bite-size pieces and enjoy now or later!

*For a substitution use any fruit-flavored vitamin powder or protein powder.

NUTRITION PER SERVING

93 Calories
2g Protein
6g Fat
9g Carbs
2g Fiber
3g Sugar

Almost Chocolate
Crème Pie Bites

Makes 12

If you've been craving chocolate cream pie, you will love these healthy treats… and you won't believe there isn't any chocolate!

INGREDIENTS

Pie Crust:
> 1 ¼ **cup** oats
> 1 **cup** water
> 1 **tbsp** agave syrup
> 1 **tsp** cinnamon

Filling:
> 3 **tbsp** Artisana Açai Berry Nut Butter*
> 3 **tbsp** plain nonfat Greek yogurt

DIRECTIONS

Preheat oven to 350 degrees. Mix pie crust ingredients well and form 12 cups in a greased mini muffin pan by using finger to indent middle of each dollop of batter. Bake for 12 minutes. Let cool and gently remove from pan. Combine filling ingredients in a bowl and mix well. Evenly fill all pie crust cups with approximately ½ tbsp filling in each. Refrigerate for one hour before serving.

*Use almond butter for a substitution.

NUTRITION PER SERVING

62 Calories
2g Protein
3g Fat
8g Carbs
1g Fiber
2g Sugar

gf v

Fiesta Dip

Serves 1

I love easy, wholesome food, and this dip is no different. It consists of three ingredients that are so simple on their own, yet make an amazing taste experience when combined.

INGREDIENTS

½ avocado
¼ **cup** black beans
¼ **cup** salsa

DIRECTIONS

Mash all ingredients with a fork in a bowl and enjoy with a healthy carb (sweet potato, quinoa, wheat pita) for a well-balanced snack or meal.

SERVING & LEFTOVER SUGGESTIONS

Serve with *Zesty Pita Chips* (p. 107).

NUTRITION PER SERVING

219 Calories
6g Protein
14g Fat
22g Carbs
11g Fiber
0g Sugar

gf df v

Healthy Key Lime Pie Bites

Makes 12

If you've been craving key lime pie, but you can't bring yourself to buy it anymore after reading the nutritional facts, this recipe is for you!

INGREDIENTS

Pie Crust:

    1 ¼ cup oats
    1 cup water
    1 tbsp agave syrup
    1 tsp cinnamon

Filling:

    4 tbsp Barlean's Omega Swirl, Key Lime
    2 tbsp plain nonfat Greek yogurt

DIRECTIONS

Preheat oven to 350 degrees. Mix crust ingredients well and form 12 cups in a greased mini muffin pan by using finger to indent middle of each dollop of batter. Bake for 12 minutes. Let cool and gently remove from pan. Combine filling ingredients in a bowl and mix well. Evenly fill all pie crust cups with approximately ½ tbsp of filling in each. Garnish with a pepita or almond slice and refrigerate for one hour before serving.

NUTRITION PER SERVING

    61 Calories
    1g Protein
    2g Fat
    9g Carbs
    1g Fiber
    0g Sugar

gf v

BAKED STUFFED RED ONION

SERVES 6-8

I love this dish because it is so unique and will impress guests and family alike!

INGREDIENTS

2	medium red onions
1 tsp	olive oil
2 tbsp	pinons
1 tbsp	fresh chopped cilantro
1 tbsp	fresh minced garlic
2 tsp	freshly ground black pepper
3 tbsp	crumbled whole wheat crackers or stale wheat bread
4 oz	reduced-fat feta cheese, crumbled

DIRECTIONS

Preheat oven to 350 degrees. Cut off both ends of each onion and remove outer skin. Boil onions in a large pot until soft, approximately 15 minutes. Remove onions from water with a slotted spoon and let cool enough to handle. Push the inner portions of the onions out one end, leaving two or three outer layers as a shell to stuff. Chop inner portions into small pieces and sauté in olive oil with nuts, cilantro, garlic, and pepper. Transfer sautéed ingredients into a mixing bowl and add bread crumbs and feta cheese. Combine. Place onion shells in a lightly oiled deep baking dish and stuff with filling. Cover loosely with aluminum foil and bake for 30 minutes, removing foil after first 20 minutes.

SERVING & LEFTOVER SUGGESTIONS

Serve warm with hearty wheat crackers or *Zesty Pita Chips* (p. 107). Mix leftovers with low-fat cottage cheese for a quick pasta stuffing and top with marinara sauce.

NUTRITION PER SERVING

68	Calories
4g	Protein
4g	Fat
5g	Carbs
1g	Fiber
0g	Sugar

gf substitute quinoa for crackers *v*

Baked Tofu & Apple Bites

Makes approximately 40

This is a party favorite! I have had so many anti-tofu people say they can't believe it's tofu.

INGREDIENTS

1 tbsp	apple cider vinegar
2 tsp each	liquid aminos (or low-sodium soy sauce), chili paste, Dijon mustard, olive oil, dried basil, garlic powder, dried onion flakes
1 5.5-oz can	low-sodium V8
1 package	extra firm tofu
1	large granny smith apple

DIRECTIONS

Wrap the tofu in clean cloths or paper towels and press the liquid out by placing a heavy object like a phone book on top for an hour or so. Preheat oven to 425 degrees. Combine all marinade ingredients in a sealable container like a glass jar or plastic bag. Cut pressed tofu into 1" cubes and add to marinade container. Tightly seal container and marinate at room temperature for an hour, turning container a few times to ensure even coverage. Pour tofu marinade onto a greased baking sheet or dish large enough to spread tofu cubes out in a single layer. Bake tofu for 50-60 minutes, turning cubes halfway through. Remove baked tofu, let cool to room temperature, and then refrigerate for 1 hour. Cut apple into bite-size pieces, slightly smaller than the tofu cubes. Pair an apple slice with a tofu cube on a toothpick, arrange on a platter, and serve.

SERVING & LEFTOVER SUGGESTIONS

Lucky you! These are awesome portable snacks; even if the apple turns brown it still tastes great and is a great protein boost.

NUTRITION PER SERVING

17 Calories
1g Protein
1g Fat
1g Carbs
0g Fiber
1g Sugar

gf (use GF soy sauce) *df* *v*

Black Bean Cilantro
Hummus

Makes 3 cups

I created this for a friend's New Year's Day brunch and it was so fun to share something healthy and delicious with her on the first day of a new year!

INGREDIENTS

1 15oz can	garbanzo beans (chick peas)
1 15oz can	black beans
4 tbsp	lime juice
2 tbsp	tahini
¼ cup	salsa
¼ cup	fresh cilantro, stems removed
1 tsp	garlic powder
1 tsp	cumin

DIRECTIONS

Rinse and drain beans well and place in food processor. Squeeze fresh lime juice into processor, add all remaining ingredients, and process on medium speed until all ingredients are well puréed. Transfer to a serving bowl, cover with plastic wrap and refrigerate for 30 minutes before serving.

SERVING & LEFTOVER SUGGESTIONS

Serve with *Zesty Pita Chips* (p. 107) or freshly cut vegetables. Stuff a whole wheat pita half with leftover hummus, adding freshly chopped tomato and sprouts for a high-energy sandwich.

NUTRITION PER SERVING

284	Calories
13g	Protein
7g	Fat
45g	Carbs
12g	Fiber
0g	Sugar

gf df v

Egg White Canapés

Makes 12

This was created at the last minute as a healthy alternative to the traditional deviled eggs served at Easter time. It was a huge hit!

INGREDIENTS

6 hard-boiled eggs, cooled and shells removed

Black Bean Filling – combine the following:
¼ cup canned black beans, rinsed and drained
1 tbsp salsa

Hummus Filling – combine the following:
¼ cup hummus
1 tbsp red bell pepper, stems and seeds removed, finely chopped

Avocado Filling – combine the following:
½ avocado, mashed
1 tsp lime juice

DIRECTIONS

Cut eggs in half lengthwise and discard yolks. Lay 12 halves on a serving platter and fill with your choice of fillings listed above. Serve immediately, or cover and refrigerate until served.

SERVING & LEFTOVER SUGGESTIONS

Serve as an evening appetizer or for Sunday brunch with *Pan-Fried Sweet Potatoes and Onions* (p. 31). Leftover filling? Combine them all for a delicious dip.

NUTRITION PER SERVING

281 Calories
41g Protein
9g Fat
8g Carbs
1g Fiber
4g Sugar

gf df v

Roasted Garbanzo Snack

Makes approximately 2 cups

This is one of my favorite snacks to make because it is so versatile and quick: a great afternoon snack, side dish, trail mix, or bar mix!

INGREDIENTS

- **1 tbsp** olive oil
- **1 tbsp** lime juice
- **2 tsp** liquid aminos (or low-sodium soy sauce)
- **1 tsp** paprika
- **1 tsp** ground thyme
- **½ tsp** cayenne pepper
- **1 15oz** can garbanzo beans (chick peas), rinsed and strained

DIRECTIONS

Preheat oven to 375 degrees. Combine all marinade ingredients in a sealable container like a glass jar or plastic bag. Add garbanzo beans to marinade container. Tightly seal container and gently turn and rotate to ensure even coverage. Pour contents onto a greased baking sheet or dish large enough to spread garbanzo beans out in a single layer. Bake for 15-20 minutes. Remove roasted garbanzo beans and let cool to room temperature before serving.

SERVING & LEFTOVER SUGGESTIONS

Try serving this healthy alternative to croutons as a salad topper, if you don't eat them all before they hit the salad! Blend leftover snack with olive oil and seasoning for a quick hummus.

NUTRITION PER SERVING

- **238** Calories
- **7g** Protein
- **9g** Fat
- **34g** Carbs
- **7g** Fiber
- **0g** Sugar

gf (use GF soy sauce) *df* *v*

ROASTED NUTS

MAKES APPROXIMATELY 2 CUPS

I remember creating this recipe when I was looking for something much easier and healthier than roasting with honey. I found that the orange peel added just enough sweetness, without any of the sugar of the honey.

INGREDIENTS

1 tbsp lime juice
1 tsp olive oil
1 tsp liquid aminos (or low-sodium soy sauce)
1 tsp paprika
1 tsp cayenne pepper
1 tsp orange peel
¼ cup each raw, unsalted almonds, walnuts, pecans, pepitas (pumpkin seeds)

DIRECTIONS

Preheat oven to 375 degrees. Combine all marinade ingredients in a sealable container like a glass jar or plastic bag. Add all nuts to marinade container. Tightly seal container and gently turn and rotate to ensure even coverage. Pour contents onto a greased baking sheet or dish large enough to spread nuts out in a single layer. Bake for 15-20 minutes. Remove roasted nuts and let cool to room temperature before serving.

SERVING & LEFTOVER SUGGESTIONS

Mix with raisins for a sweet and salty combo, or mix into your favorite natural nut butter for the most flavorful chunky nut butter you can imagine. Leftovers make a great salad topping.

NUTRITION PER SERVING

122 Calories
3g Protein
11g Fat
4g Carbs
2g Fiber
0g Sugar

gf (use GF soy sauce) *df v*

ROASTED RED PEPPER & PINON
HUMMUS

SERVES 4

I'd never thought about making any type of hummus without its main staple: tahini. But why follow the rules? The pinons and olive oil together add such a warm undertone to the subtle flavor of the roasted red pepper—I'm glad I thought outside the tahini jar for this one!

INGREDIENTS

1 can	garbanzo beans (chick peas)
1	large lime
1	whole marinated (not in oil) roasted red pepper
½ tsp	olive oil
¼ cup	pinons
¼ cup	fresh basil, stems removed
2 tsp	onion powder
2 tsp	paprika
2 tsp	minced garlic
	freshly ground black pepper, to taste

DIRECTIONS

Rinse and drain beans well and place in food processor. Squeeze fresh lime juice into processor, add all remaining ingredients, and process on medium speed until all ingredients are well pureed. Transfer to a serving bowl, cover with plastic wrap, and refrigerate for 30 minutes before serving.

SERVING & LEFTOVER SUGGESTIONS

Serve as a dip with *Zesty Pita Chips* (p. 107) or celery sticks. Stuff leftover hummus into a whole wheat pita half, adding freshly chopped tomato and sprouts for a high-energy sandwich.

NUTRITION PER SERVING

136 Calories
4g Protein
7g Fat
15g Carbs
3g Fiber
0g Sugar

gf df v

STUFFED MUSHROOM CAPS

MAKES 8

This was one of the first appetizers I created when I was looking for non-dairy options for party foods. Using hummus in the stuffing was a perfect way to get the smooth consistency I was looking for.

INGREDIENTS

8	baby bella mushrooms, washed
2 tbsp	balsamic vinegar
2 tsp	olive oil
1/4	onion, finely chopped
1 tbsp	pinions
½ cup	fresh spinach, finely chopped
1 tsp	garlic powder
1 tsp	black pepper
1 tbsp	hummus

DIRECTIONS

Preheat oven to 350 degrees. Remove stems from mushrooms and gently scoop out some of the inners of the cap. Set aside. Place caps in a small dish with half the balsamic vinegar; set aside and let marinate. Heat olive oil in a pan, add the mushroom stems and inners, as well as the remaining ingredients except the hummus. Saute on high heat for 5-8 minutes. Remove from heat and transfer to a mixing bowl. Add hummus and mix well. Fill each mushroom cap with a small and equal amount of mixture. Place filled caps in a greased baking dish and bake for 15 minutes. Remove from oven and serve warm.

SERVING & LEFTOVER SUGGESTIONS

Chop leftovers and add to quinoa or rice for an instant pilaf.

NUTRITION PER SERVING

30 Calories
1g Protein
2g Fat
2g Carbs
0g Fiber
0g Sugar

gf df v

Sweet Potato & Red Onion
Quesadilla

Serves 4-6

*Prepare for a taste bud explosion
and a great after school snack for the kids!*

INGREDIENTS

1 tsp	olive oil
1	large sweet potato
1	large red onion, finely chopped
1 tbsp	garlic powder
1 tbsp	ground paprika
4	whole wheat flour tortillas
16 oz	shredded cheddar or jack cheese

DIRECTIONS

Microwave potato on high for 90 seconds to soften but not fully cook. Leaving skin on, cut softened potato into quarters and slice each quarter into ½-inch slices. Heat olive oil in a large pan. Add potato slices, chopped onion, garlic, and paprika to the same pan and sauté on high heat for 5-8 minutes or until potatoes and onions are slightly browned. Transfer contents of pan to a bowl. Lower heat to medium. Prepare first quesadilla by placing a tortilla in the pan and sprinkling ¼ of the cheese, followed by ¼ of the vegetable mixture. Let this cook until cheese is melted, approximately 4 minutes. Using a spatula, fold one half of the tortilla over, and remove cooked quesadilla. Prepare remaining quesadilla in the same order. Let cooked quesadillas cool slightly and slice into 4 or 5 pieces each.

SERVING & LEFTOVER SUGGESTIONS

Refrigerated leftover slices in a baggie make a great protein-packed snack on the go.

NUTRITION PER SERVING

429 Calories
23g Protein
28g Fat
23g Carbs
3g Fiber
4g Sugar

v

Sweet Potato & Cranberry Pie

Serves 6-8

This delicious dish is Thanksgiving without the turkey!

INGREDIENTS

2	medium-sized sweet potatoes
8 oz	fat-free evaporated milk
2	egg whites or equivalent egg substitute
1 tbsp	brown sugar
1 tbsp	ground cinnamon
1 tsp	ground cloves
1 cup	dried cranberries or raisins
1	graham cracker-type pie crust

DIRECTIONS

Preheat oven to 425 degrees. Microwave sweet potatoes until soft—approximately 7 minutes. Remove cooked potatoes and slice open to allow them to cool enough to handle. Scoop softened potato flesh from skins into a large mixing bowl, and add all remaining ingredients for filling except cranberries, and mix on medium speed for 30-60 seconds. When all contents are well combined, fold in cranberries by hand. Pour filling into pie shell and bake for 15 minutes. Reduce heat to 425 degrees and bake another 30 minutes. Pie is done when a toothpick inserted into middle comes out dry. Remove pie from oven and allow to cool on a rack for 5-10 minutes before serving.

SERVING & LEFTOVER SUGGESTIONS

This can also be refrigerated for one hour and served cold. Cut leftover pie into small pieces that can be layered in a tall sundae glass, alternating each layer with a scoop of low-fat vanilla greek yogurt.

NUTRITION PER SERVING

281 Calories
41g Protein
9g Fat
8g Carbs
1g Fiber
4g Sugar

V

Sauces & Marinades

Four Pepper & Mango
Pico de Gallo

Serves 4

I love making this pico de gallo without tomatoes—it's a fresh spin!

INGREDIENTS

1 each red, yellow, and orange bell peppers
3 large jalapeño peppers
½ cup frozen mango chunks, thawed and diced
¼ cup thinly sliced chives
1 cup fresh cilantro, stems removed and leaves chopped
1 large lime

DIRECTIONS

After removing stems and seeds, finely chop all peppers. Place into a bowl large enough to combine with all remaining ingredients. Add diced mango, chives, and cilantro to bowl. Squeeze fresh lime juice into bowl, and mix until all ingredients are well combined. Refrigerate, covered, for 30 minutes before serving.

SERVING & LEFTOVER SUGGESTIONS

Serve on top of *Zesty Pita Chips* (p. 107), or as a garnish to any fish. Mix leftovers into an egg white omelet, or puree leftovers and eat as a cold soup.

NUTRITION PER SERVING

59 Calories
2g Protein
0g Fat
15g Carbs
2g Fiber
4g Sugar

gf df v

FRESH & EASY PIZZA SAUCE

MAKES ENOUGH SAUCE FOR 2 LARGE PIZZAS

With all the homemade pizza I make, I felt strange using store bought sauces, but didn't want to invest the time in making my homemade sauce from scratch every time. So I came up with this great quick version of homemade. While it doesn't simmer as long as some of my other sauces, it is perfect for a pizza that has many other flavors adding to the fun.

INGREDIENTS

10-15	baby bella mushrooms, finely chopped
1 tsp	olive oil
½	small red onion, finely chopped
4	garlic cloves, peeled and diced
¼ cup	balsamic vinegar
1 14.5oz can	tomato sauce
1 6oz can	tomato paste
2 tsp	crushed red pepper
½ cup	fresh basil, finely chopped
	freshly ground black pepper, to taste

DIRECTIONS

Heat oil in a medium saucepot, adding onion, mushrooms, garlic, and pepper. Saute for 5-10 minutes, adding balsamic vinegar for the last minute. Add tomato sauce, paste, and crushed red pepper to pot. Stir well, then cover and simmer for one hour, stirring occasionally. Add basil during final 10 minutes, then remove from heat and let cool before using.

SERVING & LEFTOVER SUGGESTIONS

Use as pizza sauce for *Smoky Vegetable & Pinon Pizza* (p. 103) or *Feta & Portabella Pizza* (p. 101). Add a dollop of leftover sauce to your favorite soup, or use as a spread on a melted cheese sandwich. Or, add more liquid (water or soy sauce) and use as a marinade for fish or tofu.

NUTRITION PER SERVING

252 Calories
11g Protein
4g Fat
49g Carbs
9g Fiber
22g Sugar

gf df v

Fresh Vegetable Marinade

Makes enough for a full skillet of fresh cut vegetables.

This is the foundation for so many of my dishes—these ingredients are magical together and enhance the natural flavor of real, whole foods.

INGREDIENTS

- **2 tbsp** olive oil
- **2 tbsp** apple cider vinegar
- **2 tsp** liquid aminos
- **1 tsp** crushed garlic
- **1 tsp** black pepper

DIRECTIONS

Combine all ingredients and add to chopped vegetables in a stir fry pan. Saute until cooked to preferred tenderness and enjoy.

SERVING & LEFTOVER SUGGESTIONS

Makes a delicious marinade for chicken, beef, or fish.

NUTRITION PER SERVING

- **243** Calories
- **0g** Protein
- **27g** Fat
- **2g** Carbs
- **0g** Fiber
- **2g** Sugar

gf df v

ROCKY POINT SALSA

SERVES 4-6

*This is such a fun salsa! I first had it in Rocky Point, Mexico,
with some friends. It still remains a favorite after years have passed.*

INGREDIENTS

1 28oz can	crushed tomatoes
1 cup	green onions, chopped
4	large jalapeños, chopped
½ cup	firmly packed fresh cilantro, stems removed, chopped
½ cup	peach or mango slices, peeled and chopped
5 tsp	minced garlic
4 tsp	hot taco spice mix
2 tsp	ground cumin seed
1 ½ tsp	crushed Mexican oregano
1 4oz can	chopped, roasted green chiles

DIRECTIONS

Mix all ingredients together in a large bowl. Cover and let sit at least 30 minutes before serving.

SERVING & LEFTOVER SUGGESTIONS

Serve with corn and flour tortilla chips. Top baked sweet potato with a little cottage cheese and a generous dollop of salsa.

NUTRITION PER SERVING

- **281** Calories
- **41g** Protein
- **9g** Fat
- **8g** Carbs
- **1g** Fiber
- **4g** Sugar

gf df v

BALSAMIC VINAIGRETTE

MAKES 7 SERVINGS,
ENOUGH FOR A WEEK'S WORTH OF SALADS

No need for store-bought dressing when you can create this amazing flavor in so few steps.

INGREDIENTS

- **¾ cup** balsamic vinegar
- **½ cup** olive oil
- **¼ cup** water
- **1 tbsp** Dijon mustard
- **¼ cup** salt-free seasoning

DIRECTIONS

Combine all ingredients in a jar with a tight-fitting lid and stir/shake well. Refrigerate for 30 minutes prior to serving for optimal consistency and flavor.

SERVING & LEFTOVER SUGGESTIONS

Makes a delicious marinade for chicken, beef, or fish.

NUTRITION PER SERVING

- **150** Calories
- **0g** Protein
- **15g** Fat
- **3g** Carbs
- **0g** Fiber
- **0g** Sugar

gf df v

ASIAN DRAGON DRESSING

MAKES ENOUGH FOR A FULL SKILLET
OF FRESH STIR FRY

This is a favorite of my friends at the Phoenix fire station where I cooked for them as part of my "Serving Those Who Serve Us" program.

INGREDIENTS

- **¼ cup** liquid aminos (or low-sodium soy sauce)
- **¼ cup** apple cider vinegar
- **¼ cup** Chinese mustard
- **¼ cup** fresh cilantro, finely chopped
- **1 tbsp** ground fresh chili paste

DIRECTIONS

Combine all ingredients and enjoy for an added kick to your favorite stir fry or a freshly seared ahi tuna salad.

SERVING & LEFTOVER SUGGESTIONS

Makes a delicious marinade for chicken, beef, or fish.

NUTRITION PER SERVING

- **26** Calories
- **2g** Protein
- **1g** Fat
- **3g** Carbs
- **1g** Fiber
- **0g** Sugar

gf (use GF soy sauce) *df v*

Fresh Fish Taco Sauce

Makes 1 cup

I created this recipe for a bodybuilding friend who needed a healthy alternative to tartar sauce.

INGREDIENTS

¾ cup plain nonfat Greek yogurt
1 tbsp lime juice
¼ cup Dijon mustard
¼ cup fresh cilantro, finely chopped

DIRECTIONS

Whisk all ingredients in a mixing bowl and refrigerate until used.

SERVING & LEFTOVER SUGGESTIONS

Drizzle on *Healthy Fish Tacos* (p. 83) and enjoy! Leftovers make a delicious salad dressing or sauce for leftover brown rice.

NUTRITION PER SERVING

121 Calories
18g Protein
2g Fat
11g Carbs
2g Fiber
6g Sugar

SPICY FISH TACO SAUCE

MAKES 1 CUP

A bodybuilding friend of mine asked for some help getting over his intense cravings for fish tacos right before a contest. He had a healthy version all figured out, except for the traditional creamy sauce that he loved so much. So I made this for him and besides staying on his diet, he now has a new favorite sauce!

INGREDIENTS

¾ cup plain nonfat Greek yogurt
1 tbsp lime juice
¼ cup salsa
¼ cup fresh cilantro, finely chopped

DIRECTIONS

Whisk all ingredients in a mixing bowl and refrigerate until used.

SERVING & LEFTOVER SUGGESTIONS

Drizzle on *Healthy Fish Tacos* (p. 83) and enjoy! Leftovers make a delicious salad dressing or sauce.

NUTRITION PER SERVING

121 Calories
18g Protein
2g Fat
11g Carbs
2g Fiber
6g Sugar

gf v

HUMMUS VINAIGRETTE

MAKES ENOUGH FOR
A WEEK'S WORTH OF SALADS

Craving creamy dressing? This one is creamy, yet healthy!

INGREDIENTS

½ **cup** apple cider vinegar
½ **cup** olive oil
¾ **cup** hummus
¼ **cup** salt-free seasoning

DIRECTIONS

Combine all ingredients in a jar with a tight-fitting lid and stir/shake well. Refrigerate for 30 minutes prior to serving for optimal consistency and flavor.

SERVING & LEFTOVER SUGGESTIONS

Add to leftover veggies or rice pilaf for a leftover makeover!

NUTRITION PER SERVING

196 Calories
2g Protein
21g Fat
3g Carbs
1g Fiber
0g Sugar

gf df v

SPICY MARINARA SAUCE

MAKES APPROXIMATELY 8 CUPS

The sauce is the star of every Italian meal, and this one keeps winning the Emmy in my house.

INGREDIENTS

2 tsp	olive oil
1	small red onion, chopped
½ cup	balsamic vinegar
1 28oz can	natural tomato puree
1 28oz can	natural whole plum tomatoes
1 14.5oz can	natural tomato sauce
1 6oz can	natural tomato paste
4 cups	water
4 cubes	vegetable bouillon (enough for 4 cups of broth)
1 cup	white wine
4 tbsp	garlic powder
2 tbsp	dried crushed basil
3 tbsp	crushed red pepper
½ cup	fresh chopped basil
1 tsp	crushed oregano
	freshly ground black pepper to taste

DIRECTIONS

Heat oil in a large sauce pot. Saute onion for 5-10 minutes, adding balsamic vinegar for the last minute. Add all remaining ingredients except the basil and oregano to pot. Bring to a boil, then reduce heat to simmer and cover. Continue to slow cook the sauce for one hour. Add basil and oregano; mix well. Simmer another 10 minutes, then turn off heat. Let covered pot sit for 30 minutes before serving to allow flavors to marry and sauce to cool.

Special note: this sauce tastes best the next day, so consider preparing it the day before your meal and reheat to serve.

SERVING & LEFTOVER SUGGESTIONS

Serve with any pasta dish. Use leftovers to top your favorite soup, or as a spread on a melted cheese sandwich. Or add more liquid (water or soy sauce) and use as a marinade for fish or tofu.

NUTRITION PER SERVING

105 Calories
3g Protein
2g Fat
15g Carbs
3g Fiber
8g Sugar

gf df v

SPICY SALSA DRESSING

MAKES 7 SERVINGS,
ENOUGH FOR A WEEK'S WORTH OF SALADS

I remember being in Jamaica, piling a big plate of fresh food from the salad bar, and then hitting a wall at the dressings. The only options were cream based dressings which are not for me, and they did not offer oil and vinegar. So I went to the fajita bar and put the fresh salsa on my salad. That was the first time I tried salsa on salad and loved it so much that I incorporate it often at home.

INGREDIENTS

- **½ cup** apple cider vinegar
- **½ cup** olive oil
- **¾ cup** chunky salsa
- **¼ cup** plain nonfat Greek yogurt
- **¼ cup** fresh cilantro, finely chopped

DIRECTIONS

Combine all ingredients in a jar with a tight-fitting lid and stir/shake well. Refrigerate for 30 minutes prior to serving for optimal consistency and flavor.

SERVING & LEFTOVER SUGGESTIONS

Makes a delicious marinade for chicken, beef, or fish.

NUTRITION PER SERVING

- **150** Calories
- **1g** Protein
- **15g** Fat
- **3g** Carbs
- **1g** Fiber
- **1g** Sugar

gf v

Workout Foods

Greenest Power Shake

Typical blender-full serves 2

*It's amazing how all things green come together in this smoothie—
with just a little help from its friends banana and protein—to taste
so sweet, delicious, and clean.*

INGREDIENTS

½	frozen banana, skin removed
½	avocado
2 scoops	vanilla protein powder
1 cup	fresh spinach leaves
1 cup	chilled green tea
10	fresh mint leaves
1 cup	ice cubes

DIRECTIONS

Add all ingredients to blender, leaving 1 inch of room at the top. Secure lid and blend on medium to high speed until all contents are smooth, but not liquefied. Pour and enjoy.

NUTRITION PER SERVING

196	Calories
21g	Protein
8g	Fat
13g	Carbs
3g	Fiber
5g	Sugar

gf df v

I'VE GOT THE POWER
COOKIES

YIELDS 36 SMALL COOKIES

A cookie with protein, healthy fat, and complex carbs all in one treat for the serious athlete!

INGREDIENTS

- **1 cup** almond flour
- **1 cup** quinoa flour
- **2 cups** oats
- **¼ cup** ground flax meal
- **1 tbsp** cinnamon
- **3 scoops** vanilla protein powder
- **1 cup** chopped walnuts
- **2 tsp** minced ginger
- **½ cup** Lighter Bake (or other fruit puree)
- **4 large** egg whites
- **1 cup** water

DIRECTIONS

Preheat oven to 370 degrees. Mix all ingredients until they have a smooth, consistent texture. Using rounded tablespoon, drop batter onto well-oiled (or parchment paper) cookie sheets. Bake for 10 minutes. Remove from heat, let cool, and store in dry, airtight container.

SERVING & LEFTOVER SUGGESTIONS

Crumble cookies onto low-fat Greek yogurt and add fresh fruit and cinnamon for a delicious parfait.

NUTRITION PER SERVING

76 Calories
4g Protein
4g Fat
6g Carbs
1g Fiber
0g Sugar

gf df v

Popeye Power Shake

Typical blender-full serves 2

*This is my all-time favorite smoothie combination: delicious, simple, healthy.
Plus it gives me a head start on my veggie consumption for the day!*

INGREDIENTS

1	frozen banana, skin removed*
6-8	frozen strawberries*
1 cup	plain nonfat Greek yogurt
2 tbsp	almond butter
½ cup	protein powder (vanilla recommended)
1 tbsp	ground cinnamon
1 cup	fresh spinach leaves, stems removed
1 cup	water

DIRECTIONS

*Many ready-to-use options are available in the freezer section of your grocery store; alternatively any fresh fruit that starts to become too ripe can be peeled, placed in a freezer bag, and frozen for later use.

Add all ingredients to blender, leaving 1 inch of room at the top. Secure lid and blend on medium to high speed until all contents are smooth, but not liquefied. Pour and enjoy.

NUTRITION PER SERVING

309 Calories
28g Protein
11g Fat
29g Carbs
7g Fiber
16g Sugar

gf df substitute almond milk for yogurt *v*

BERRY SMOOTHIE

TYPICAL BLENDER-FULL SERVES 2

Kids love this smoothie!

INGREDIENTS

½	frozen banana, skin removed*
4-6	frozen strawberries*
½ cup	frozen blueberries*
1 cup	plain nonfat Greek yogurt
2 scoops	protein powder (vanilla recommended)
1 tbsp	ground cinnamon
1 cup	water
½ cup	ice cubes

DIRECTIONS

*Many ready-to-use options are available in the freezer section of your grocery store; alternatively any fresh fruit that starts to become too ripe can be peeled, placed in a freezer bag, and frozen for later use.

Add all ingredients to blender, leaving 1 inch of room at the top. Secure lid and blend on medium to high speed until all contents are smooth, but not liquefied. Pour and enjoy.

NUTRITION PER SERVING

243	Calories
37g	Protein
2g	Fat
21g	Carbs
2g	Fiber
13g	Sugar

gf df substitute almond milk for yogurt *v*

Oatmeal Cookie Smoothie

Typical blender-full serves 2

Okay, this smoothie is deadly and tastes too good to share! You will not believe how rich and creamy the avocado makes the smoothie!

INGREDIENTS

½	avocado, skin removed
¾ cup	dry oats
2 scoops	vanilla protein powder
½ cup	all-natural apple sauce
1 tbsp	ground cinnamon
1 tsp	ground nutmeg
1 cup	water
½ cup	ice cubes

DIRECTIONS

Add all ingredients to blender, leaving 1 inch of room at the top. Secure lid and blend on medium to high speed until all contents are smooth, but not liquefied. Pour and enjoy.

NUTRITION PER SERVING

333	Calories
25g	Protein
12g	Fat
34g	Carbs
8g	Fiber
7g	Sugar

gf df v

PROTEIN BROWNIES

YIELDS 12 SMALL BROWNIES

A brownie with protein, healthy fat, and complex carbs for the serious athlete who deserves a treat!

INGREDIENTS

1 cup	oats
½ cup	canned natural pumpkin (no sugar added)
2 tbsp	ground flax meal
1 tbsp	cinnamon
3 scoops	chocolate protein powder
1 tbsp	almond butter
4	egg whites
¼ cup	water
1 tsp	baking powder
1 packet	Stevia or other natural sweetener

DIRECTIONS

Preheat oven to 360 degrees. Mix all ingredients until they have a smooth, consistent texture. Pour batter into well-oiled baking dish. Bake for 15-20 minutes. Remove from oven, let cool, cut into 12 squares, and store in dry, airtight container.

SERVING & LEFTOVER SUGGESTIONS

Crumble leftover brownie bits into low-fat Greek yogurt and add fresh fruit and cinnamon for a delicious parfait.

NUTRITION PER SERVING

74	Calories
7g	Protein
2g	Fat
7g	Carbs
2g	Fiber
1g	Sugar

gf df v

TURKEY APPLE POWER CAKES

MAKES 9

I am always looking for a way to eat on the run—this is a great addition to my arsenal!

INGREDIENTS

1	medium sweet potato with skin, microwaved to soften, cut into small pieces
1 cup	garbanzo beans (chick peas), mashed with a fork
1	medium green apple, diced with skin on
8oz	pre-cooked turkey breast, diced or shredded
2	egg whites
2 tbsp	quinoa, oat, or wheat flour
¼ cup	fresh parsley, finely chopped
1 tbsp	crushed rosemary
1 tbsp	salt-free mixed seasoning
1 tsp	black pepper

DIRECTIONS

Preheat oven to 375 degrees. Combine all ingredients in a mixing bowl until they have a smooth, slightly moist consistency. Add another egg white if texture is too dry. Roll mixture into 9 balls and place on well-oiled baking sheet. Flatten each ball into a round, half-inch thick power cake and bake for 25 minutes, turning over after 15 minutes. Remove from oven and let cool before serving or storing.

SERVING & LEFTOVER SUGGESTIONS

These make great mini meals when on the go at work, school, sports, or travel. Crumble leftovers for a salad topper with healthy protein and carbs.

NUTRITION PER SERVING

91	Calories
7g	Protein
1g	Fat
14g	Carbs
3g	Fiber
4g	Sugar

gf (no wheat flour) *df*

CLEAN CARB SNACK CAKES

MAKES 9

I created this recipe when I was in a carb-load cycle for bodybuilding training. It's a delicious and easy way to eat healthy, complex carbs on the go!

INGREDIENTS

- **1** medium sweet potato, skin on, grated
- **1 cup** canned black beans, rinsed and drained
- **1 cup** cooked quinoa
- **2** egg whites
- **2 tbsp** quinoa, oat, or wheat flour
- **¼ cup** fresh cilantro or parsley, finely chopped
- **1 tbsp** salt-free mixed seasoning
- **1 tsp** cayenne pepper

DIRECTIONS

Preheat oven to 375 degrees. Combine all ingredients in a mixing bowl until they have a smooth, slightly moist consistency. Add another egg white if texture is too dry. Roll mixture into 9 balls and place on well-oiled baking sheet. Flatten each ball into a round, half-inch thick snack cake and bake for 25 minutes, turning over after 15 minutes. Remove from oven and let cool before serving or storing.

SERVING & LEFTOVER SUGGESTIONS

Crumble leftovers and add to lean ground turkey for a hearty, healthy burger patty.

NUTRITION PER SERVING

- **83** Calories
- **4g** Protein
- **1g** Fat
- **15g** Carbs
- **3g** Fiber
- **1g** Sugar

gf (no wheat flour) *df v*

CHOCOLATE PEANUT BUTTER SMOOTHIE

TYPICAL BLENDER-FULL SERVES 2

This has become a staple treat for me when I have a sweet tooth that won't go away. Not to mention a great breakfast shake on days that I don't have time for an egg breakfast.

INGREDIENTS

1 cup	fresh spinach
1	banana
2 scoops	chocolate protein powder
1 tbsp	ground flaxseed
1 tbsp	almond butter
1 cup	water
½ cup	ice cubes

DIRECTIONS

Add all ingredients to blender, leaving 1 inch of room at the top. Secure lid and blend on medium to high speed until all contents are smooth, but not liquefied. Pour and enjoy.

NUTRITION PER SERVING

205	Calories
26g	Protein
5g	Fat
19g	Carbs
5g	Fiber
8g	Sugar

gf df v

Index

Y

Yogurt

About the Author

Jen Arricale (pronounced "ah-ri-KAHL-ay") is an advocate for healthy eating while enjoying life. Having previously spent 20 years as a financial executive with Fortune 500 companies, Jen understands the challenges and benefits of nurturing a healthy self while living a busy life. As a fitness chef, champion natural physique competitor, published author, and accomplished marathoner, Jen teaches corporations, groups, and individuals how to eat healthy without sacrificing a fun, full, and balanced life. Jen shares her passion and talents through television and film, public speaking, publications, videos, blogs, and newsletters.

Jen's passion to share the comfort and happiness she found in something so simple—loving oneself with healthy food—has become the focus of her time, energy, and thoughts. Jen's recipes and preparation methods result in delicious meals with little fuss, and always reflect a healthy, balanced approach to food and life. In Jen's words, the most important thing of all is to **"love yourself, love your life, spread it around!"**

Follow Jen for daily information and inspiration: www.jenarricale.com

Shopping for Health

Jen-ify it!

+Green List

FRESH VEGETABLES
*Fresh is best and please eat in abundance! Vegetables should be your #1 priority.

- Red, orange & green bell peppers
- Cucumbers
- Mushrooms
- Broccoli
- Asparagus
- Celery
- Spinach & kale
- Tomatoes
- Red onions
- Red cabbage
- Cauliflower
- Sweet potatoes
- Zucchini

FRESH FRUITS
*Not to be eaten in abundance. Berries have the most nutrients & fiber per serving.

- Pears
- Grapefruit
- Apples
- Kiwi
- Berries
- Avocados

FROZEN FOODS
*Keep frozen vegetables on hand, they can be added to any meal to help lower your calorie intake.

- Mixed veggies or stir-fry blend
- Spinach & kale
- Red, orange & green bell peppers
- Edamame
- Frozen berries
- Grilled chicken strips (for emergency)
- Raw natural chicken breast, pork tenderloin, top sirloin & fish

CONDIMENTS, SALAD DRESSINGS & SPICES
*Calories in traditional condiments & toppings add up faster than you can imagine, so stick to home-made dressings.

- Olive & coconut oil
- Vinegars: apple cider, red wine & balsamic
- No salt seasoning
- Mustard
- Low-sugar ketchup
- Hot sauce
- Salsa (fresh is best)
- Braggs liquid aminos or low-sodium soy sauce
- Non-fat plain Greek yogurt
- Hummus (fresh is best)

GRAINS, CEREALS, & NUTS
*Enjoy with more moderation. This category is higher in calories & has less nutrients per ounce than most. Always choose unsalted & unroasted nuts when possible.

- Instant oats (unflavored) or steel cut
- Quinoa
- Brown rice
- Whole grain tortillas or wraps
- Whole wheat pita
- Whole wheat pasta
- Ezekial sprouted grain bread
- Flaxseed meal
- Raw unsalted nuts (almonds, pecans & walnuts)

Visit my website for tips on how to simply & creatively use these ingredients:

www.jenarricale.com

CANNED FOODS
*Nice things to have on hand for recipes.

- Unsweetened applesauce
- Natural peanut or nut butters
- Almond milk
- Unflavored black or garbanzo beans
- Tuna fish (in water)
- Natural salsa
- Natural pasta sauce
- Low-sodium vegetable juice

MEATS, FISH & DAIRY
- *The less dairy consumed, the faster the results. Natural meat is the best choice when possible.
- Natural chicken breast, pork tenderloin, top sirloin & fish
- Ground turkey
- Natural oven-roasted turkey breast
- Eggs
- Low-fat cottage cheese
- Low-fat mozzarella cheese
- Parmesan cheese
- Non-fat plain Greek yogurt
- Low-fat feta cheese

BEVERAGES
*Diet products are not better, stick to water!

- Bottled water, nothing added
- Sparkling water
- No-calorie flavored seltzer
- 100% fruit juices (treat for kids)
- Unsweetened green tea

Love Yourself, Love Your Life, Spread it Around